Extreme Intensity
Science-Based Programs To Maximize Muscle Growth
By David Groscup
'DR HIT'
Author Of 13 Best-Selling Bodybuilding Books
IART CFC, IART/Med-Ex High Intensity Trainer

http://drhitshighintensitybodybuilding.blogspot.com/
https://drhitscomplete9bookseries.blogspot.com/

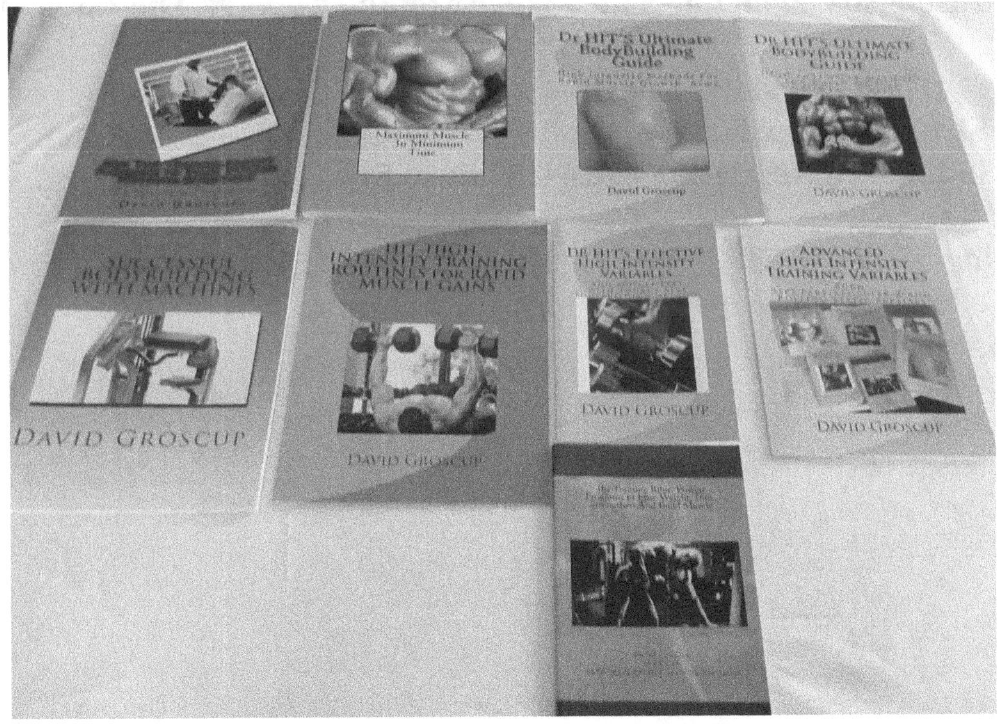

Nine of my books are available as a single master Ebook. See
https://drhitscomplete9bookseries.blogspot.com/

Contents

Introduction

This new volume on high intensity training for new muscle mass is the result of my many years of training successfully in bodybuilding. But it wasn't always that way. I wasted years training with excessive high volume training routines that were promoted as being 'sure-fire' winners at adding muscle fast.

In the beginning,virtually any bodybuilding training program yields results. This is due to new stimulus being provided to muscles that aren't used to resistance training. Once several months of steady training pass by, gains usually slow down and after more time goes by, stop altogether. Why? The muscles have become accustomed to the stress levels they're subjected to and need more intensity to drive them to adapt by adding more muscle to their girth.

The question then becomes-how do we do this? The traditional answer is to add sets, exercises and reps to increase the workload. This only leads to over-training and more stagnation-or worse yet-loss of gains!

HIT advocates,such as myself, will tell you to reduce the set count, increase the intensity of effort and add HIT variables, such as forced reps,negatives and the like. While this will yield great gains, what is needed is a variation in intensity of effort. Believe it or not, the muscles become acclimated to even extreme intensity and will stop growing. Many things can be done here. First, one or more of the many HIT variables can be added to a set, rep count can be changed, different exercises can be used, shocking programs can be done for a short time or the level of intensity can be cycled. All of these will accomplish the re-institution of muscle growth by giving muscles exposure to stress levels they're not accustomed to.

While most gains will come during the high intensity phase, the other phases, such as de-loading, are equally important as they 'de-condition' the muscles from the high intensity portion. This makes the high intensity level much more effective than it normally would be if de-loading wasn't done.

Extreme HIT Training builds on the previous books I've written on the incredibly effective form of bodybuilding training known as HIT, or High Intensity Training. As a contrast to high volume,traditional bodybuilding training which involves the use of numerous sets of many different exercises to train each,individual muscle group, High Intensity training relies on a very high level of effort during the execution of an exercise to achieve maximum growth stimulation of a muscle using a single set of each exercise.

Usually, only 2-3 exercises,consisting of one set each, are used during a training session

to provide thorough training of a muscle. Smaller muscles like biceps,shoulders and   4
triceps are trained with a total of two sets,while chest,back and legs are trained with 2-3.

With most bodybuilders completing 15-25 sets per muscle group during their workouts,
there must be a distinct difference in the way a HIT bodybuilder trains to effect enough
growth stimulation on a muscle with only 2-3 sets. The higher volume training
necessitates bodybuilders to "pace" themselves to allow completion of the high set
volume. With high intensity training, 100%, all-out effort is used to "damage" the
muscle , using the correct exercise volume, allowing maximum training effect while
avoiding over training.

While there have been many scientific advances in the field of fitness and bodybuilding,
unfortunately many bodybuilders are "stuck" using training methods that have been
proven to be inefficient at building muscle and end up inhibiting their gains.

This book will outline advanced, scientifically-based HIT techniques and strategies to
develop your muscle size and strength much faster than ever before. Maybe you've been
training for ten years or maybe ten months. Regardless of training experience,
thoroughly read this book and put the information to use in your workouts and you will
be amazed at the results.

Extreme Intensity Training

We will be using multiple intensity techniques,or variables, to increase the intensity to
such a high level so as to completely exhaust a muscle using a single set of one exercise
and no more. During the extreme intensity portion of the text, techniques will used to
reach very high intensity levels, enabling the use of a single total set to train biceps,
triceps,delts,calves and other small muscles. Larger muscles, such as back,chest and legs
will only require a total of one set also. Hang on!

Due to the extremely high intensity of this type of training, it is very important to train
with the proper frequency to avoid overtaxing both the individual muscle and the overall
central nervous system. If not kept in check, over-training will cause stagnation, if not a
loss of gains, and many times, cessation of training altogether.

Since High Intensity Training has a virtual treasure chest of different techniques to
drastically increase a bodybuilder's muscle gains, it is impossible to become stale in
your training if intensity techniques are applied properly.

As Dr. Selye stated in his book The Stress of Life, "Many people believe that, after they
have exposed themselves to very stressful activities, a rest can restore them to where
they were before. This is false. Experiments on animals have clearly shown that each

exposure leaves an indelible scar, in that it uses up reserves of adaptability which cannot be replaced.

It is true that immediately after some harassing experience, rest can restore us almost to the original level of fitness by eliminating acute fatigue. But the emphasis is on the word almost. Since we constantly go through periods of stress and rest during life, even a minute deficit of adaptation energy every day adds up -- it adds up to what we call aging."

Why High Volume Training Doesn't Work

The most popular form of bodybuilding training is high volume. It's done by almost all pro bodybuilders and most amateur and non-competitive bodybuilders. So who am I to tell you that it doesn't work? To be clear it obviously does work to a degree or no-one would use it. Countless bodybuilders and weight trainees have been using high set counts in their training for decades with good results.

The problem arises when the body becomes used to the training, the bodybuilder adds additional sets and goes into a state of over-training. First the gains stop, then enthusiasm wains due to stalled gains and he/she quits out of frustration.

To see what the problem is we need to take a look at what makes a muscle grow. It isn't marathon sessions in the gym or force-feeding protein to it in the hope it magically grows. Scientific research has shown its the amount of stress a muscle is subjected to during resistance training. If the level of effort is high enough, and the volume is limited, gains will come. The issue is the determination of the ideal amount of stress, or intensity, to use during our workouts to stimulate the maximum amount of muscle growth with the least amount of training time. Why? All training extracts energy and resources from the body's central nervous system, or CNS.

The key is to utilize just enough energy output to stimulate the muscles while avoiding excessive energy use. Experience has shown HIT, or high intensity training done properly to be ideal.

This guideline takes into consideration that muscles like biceps and triceps are small and need limited training while the back is sectional: the top portion consists of the traps and upper back muscles, the middle consists of the lats and rhomboids and the lower back the large paired muscles in the lower back (erector spinae), which help hold up the spine, and gluteal muscles. The flexor muscles are attached to the anterior (front) of the spine(which includes the abdominal muscles) and enable flexing, bending forward, lifting, and arching the lower back, therefore the back will need an additional exercise or two.

All exercises should consist of one working set each taken to momentary muscular failure with the training totals for each muscle group mentioned above.

This book takes these guidelines to the extreme by adding 2-3 HIT variables to the working set allowing total training volume to reduced to one set for each muscle group. The initial training routines will be to failure followed by standard HIT routines with variables such as forced reps or negatives, rest-pause and such, and the final routines will combine intensity techniques to reach extreme intensity.

So hang on for the ride and experience new muscle growth!

The Phases Of Muscle Growth

What are the essentials needed to bring on muscle hypertrophy? A simple answer would be to work against a sufficient load (70-85% of a 1RM) for adequate training time, and to maintain proper form to keep momentum out of the equation and sustain tension on the muscles without any noticeable unloading caused from excessive momentum. When looking at different methods, dynamic activity is superior to isometric, or stationary activity.

Each day of our lives produces evidence of periods of adaptation. We respond to the effects of the sun by tanning; we adapt to exercise in positive and negative ways, depending on the degree of the stimulus; and we adapt to life in general by acquiring new habits and knowledge. The degree to which a person responds to training can vary significantly, which is why obtaining average results in strength training research offers little advice or recommendations to trainers looking to personalize a training program for a specific individual. In power-lifting, a great focus has been placed on neurological adaptation, and a greater skill component and its effect on the success of the competing lifter. It has been suggested that neurological elements are a factor during the beginning stages of training only.

Since the role of neural factors may lessen, the nature of its role changes and becomes more focused. The more muscle and strength a bodybuilder obtains, the more unwilling the body is to add more muscle and strength; and the more a bodybuilder duplicates the same exercises in the same form of training, the more refined the skills to perform the movements becomes.

To experience an increase in the size of a muscle, three situations must occur. The first, muscle growth stimulation must occur as a result of a brief, intense workout session. The second, recovery, must be allowed to happen during proper rest periods. This means the proper frequency of training must be followed. While there are basic guidelines to follow, every individual is different, therefore experimentation must take place and a specific guidelines followed. There are two areas to focus on with regard to rest and recuperation. The first is the muscle(s) being trained and the second is the body's central nervous system.

A muscle must be fully rested prior to training again or it will be unable to generate the intensity of effort to effectively train. Since muscles are affected by exercises that focus on them specifically, they will continue to recuperate if other muscles are trained without involving their use. The CNS is depleted any time any part of the body is trained, therefore its important to have the entire body completely recovered prior to your next workout. Typically, bodybuilders who practice HIT should train each muscle once every 7-10 days, but each individual is different, so experiment to determine the precise level of rest needed.

The final phase is the growth process itself, which occurs after the body, including the CNS are fully recovered. The body will overcompensate in response to the intense stimulus it was subjected to, building an extra supply of muscle to attempt to ready itself for the next onslaught. While muscle growth takes place during relaxation, much of it happens while you are sleeping.

The Importance Of Intensity During Training

Muscle growth is dependent on the use of a high level of intensity while training. The higher the intensity level,the greater the growth stimulation. It is impossible to train for a long period of time and have the required intensity level to cause the maximum amount of muscle growth to take place. Either you train long,with a high amount of volume or you train more intensely with a much more limited volume.

Unfortunately, training intensity is often misunderstood. Articles in bodybuilding magazines usually equate intensity with the addition of sets of an exercise or the level of the resistance or training load. Neither is correct. Intensity is the level of exertion a bodybuilder puts forth during a set of an exercise. If you were to set a goal of 5 sets of barbell curls and 4 sets of concentration curls during your biceps training, it would be necessary to pace yourself to enable completion of that work. Each set would be sub-failure as a result and wouldn't expose the biceps to the proper stress level needed for maximum growth. Keep in mind that high volume training does stress the muscles with some degree of muscle-building stimulation or none of the HVT advocates would be developed.

But one must ask themselves if HVT , while leading to advanced muscular development, is the most efficient method to utilize for training. Is it better to do a total of 10-20 sets per muscle group while pacing oneself, or do a total of 1-3 sets total using a hard,intense form of training? HVT is much more likely to lead to over-training due to the high volume of training. But what level of intensity is enough or ideal? While it is virtually impossible to accurately measure the level of intensity, i.e. training at 30,40 or 100% intensity levels, push yourself as hard as you possibly can, preferably under the supervision of an experienced HIT trainer to guide you, and you will have trained with sufficient effort to grow new muscle.

The Reason "The Feel" Of The Workout Doesn't Mean It Was Effective

Does the way your muscle feel after a workout dictate how successful you were in developing sufficient stimulus to cause your muscles to grow? Not necessarily. While delayed soreness is an indication of micro tears in muscle, which are necessary to cause the body to overcompensate and build more muscle tissue after a workout, it doesn't indicate if proper training protocols were followed during the workout.

For instance, one could get on a stationary cycle and peddle at a moderate pace for an extended period of time and get sore in the leg muscles a day or two later. But that training does little to build muscle. It will build endurance but offers insufficient resistance to stimulate muscle growth. The trick is to find the proper intensity level,number of reps or time under tension and resistance level to use in your training to get optimum results. One of the ways to do this is to do an analysis of muscle fiber content in each muscle group. That way you will be able to use the proper tut for each muscle group. A muscle fiber analysis is done in the following way:

Select an isolation exercise and strictly perform an arbitrary number of repetitions at a moderate to slow speed, e.g., 6-12 repetitions, at about a 5/5 cadence (make certain the TUT is at least 60 seconds; rest approximately three minutes then complete a second set of that exercise with the same weight. In both sets train to muscular failure and record your TUT. If the TUT in the second set is 50% or less than the first set, that muscle group is predominantly fast twitch (since the muscle lost so much strength). If you lose less than 15% TUT, maintained or even increased your TUT in the second set (which is possible), that muscle group is predominantly slow twitch.

Anything between these two figures represent a mixed fiber type, whose ratios reflect the degree of TUT reduction. Now that you have determined muscle fiber type and ideal tut, or number of reps,whichever method you use, it is time to develop an ideal training regimen to maximize muscular development. If your muscle is mostly fast twitch, use a tut of 45-60 seconds per set. If it is slow twitch, use a tut of 90-120 seconds. If it falls in-between use a tut of 65-90 seconds.

Some important points to take away from this is to use:

- ideal tut or reps for each muscle fiber type/group
- proper amount of resistance to cause muscular failure or exhaustion with this rep count
- constantly attempt to use more weight every workout
- get the proper amount of rest
- train the right amount and none extra to avoid over training

How Intensity Variables Impact Total Set Count

The total number of sets given in this book are a basic guideline and are subject to the experience of the bodybuilder and his/her ability to generate a high level of intensity. HIT variables, as explained in my two books on the subject, <u>DR. HIT's Effective High Intensity Variables and Advanced High Intensity Variables</u>, are techniques either added to the end of a set or are a variation in the way a set, or exercise is performed.

For example, if a trainee does a set off barbell curls to failure (when no more reps can be performed) but desires to increase the intensity beyond failure, he/she can complete 3-4 additional reps with the assistance of a training partner. The partner would let the trainee do the majority of the lifting and just places two fingers on the bar, lifting just enough to allow completion.

Other variables like negative reps can be done in substitution of standard reps. To do these load the bar with a weight 140% of the amount typically used in a given exercise. Have a partner lift the weight to the final position of a movement and transfer the weight to you. Lower the weight under control to a count of eight. If no training partner is available negative-accentuated reps can be used in their place. Load the bar or machine with a weight 110-120% of typical weight. Lift the weight normally and lower the weight with either your left arm , as in the machine press, or left leg, as in the leg press exclusively. Repeat, lowering the weight with the opposite side.

Cycling Training Intensity To Increase Muscle Mass

Every bodybuilder has experienced burnout with their training at some point. You train as hard as you can and do all of the right exercises-but still don't build as much muscle as you should be. Why? You may be doing the same type of training day in and day out, your body has gotten used to it and made the proper adjustment to avoid adding any muscle to your frame. Your body is very adept at avoiding the addition of muscle.

The addition and maintenance of muscle is very costly to the body's systems both in energy expended to produce new muscle and energy to maintain it. We need to change our workouts from ones that have become stale from overuse and re-invigorate them into result-producing ones.

One of the best strategies to do this is the intensity variation principle. To do this we will divide your training schedule into sections. The initial section is one in which exercises are terminated when reaching mild difficulty. For example, during a set of curls using a weight that you can grind out 10 reps, you finish at eight. Rest between sets is 1-2 minutes and total sets per muscle group is 3-4 for small muscles and 4-6 for large ones. I <u>consider this period one of low growth.</u> Limit the use of this principle to once per year or you won't be benefiting from high intensity training because you'll be doing an excessive amount of inefficient higher volume training.

Here is a sample workout for Chest:

dumbbell flyes-2x12
machine dips-2x8
incline bench press-2x6

Legs:

squats-2x12
leg extensions-2x15
stiff legged dead-lifts-2x15

Back:

stiff-arm pull-downs-2x12
barbell rows-2x12
dead-lifts-2x10

Shoulder :

seated lateral raises-2x12
barbell presses-2x10

Biceps:

concentration curls-2x10
barbell curls-2x12

Triceps:

close-grip bench press-2x12
cable press-downs-2x10

After three weeks, increase the intensity of your sets by finishing them when no additional reps can be completed. In other words, if you are capable of completing 10 reps in the barbell curl with a given weight end the set there. Since the intensity has been increased, reduce the set count to 1-2 for small muscles and 2-3 for large ones. Rest no longer than 15-20 seconds between sets.

Here is a sample workout for Back:

dumbbell bench pull-overs-1x15
incline bench rows-1x12
seated medium-grip pull-downs-1x10

Chest:

pek flyes-1x12
incline machine bench presses-1x10

Legs:

leg presses-1x12
seated leg curls-1x12
calf presses-1x15

Shoulders:

dumbbell front raises-1x12
seated dumbbell presses-1x10

Biceps:

machine curls-1x10
cable palms-facing pull-downs-1x12

Triceps:

seated dumbbell extensions-1x12
close-grip machine bench presses-1x10

After an additional three weeks progress to the highest level of intensity. To maximize intensity end all sets when unable to grind out even one rep. Add intensity variables such as negative-accentuated, negative and forced reps. Negative-accentuated reps are great for bodybuilders training without a partner. They allow a trainee to experience the benefits of pure negative training safely. To do them using the leg press, press the footplate with both legs but resist the downward movement using your left leg only. Press the footplate with both legs and resist the negative with your right leg. Continue in this manner until the set is ended.

Pure negative reps need to be done with a partner. He/she raises the weight and transfers it to you. You lower the weight, usually to a count of eight before repeating. Negatives are great for building new strength and size when hitting a plateau. As mentioned before, forced reps allow effort to progress beyond the point of typical failure. After reaching failure during a set your partner applies just enough assistance to allow completion of additional reps.

A sample workout for Biceps:

dumbbell concentration curls-1x8+3 forced reps
seated palms-facing pull-downs-1x10+4 negative reps

Specificity of Training

The results you attain from your training depends heavily on the type of training you do. This is referred to as the SAID principle, or specific adaptation to imposed demands, and should help you in forming your own approach to training. For instance, if you are interested in improving your endurance , you would use an exercise regimen that would stimulate your muscle's slow-twitch fibers. This could include sets of an exercise with a high rep count and aerobic training on treadmills and cycles using brief rest periods.

Exercise training principles are based on overload, recovery, progression, reversibility and specificity. The principle of specificity is especially important if you are exercising to achieve a particular goal such as increased strength or improved aerobic fitness. Exercise is a form of stress. Your body adapts to the stresses you place upon it. This is the essence of specificity. Another term used in exercise science is SAID -- Specific Adaptations to Imposed Demands. This principle states your body will get better at the type of exercise you choose to do. The physiological adaptations you experience as a result of regular exercise depend on the type of exercise you perform.

Similar exercises stress your body in different ways. If you desire to improve your ability to run long distances, you may use cycling to offer an alternative way of training. While cycling and running offer many similar benefits, they use your muscles in differing ways. Cardiovascular fitness gained through cycling will not completely transfer to running, and benefits gained through running will not entirely transfer to cycling.

The same applies to resistance training exercises. Increasing your ability to leg press heavy weights will have minimal impact on your proficiency in the squat. Even though the movement patterns are similar, they are different enough that benefits from one will not completely transfer to the other. If looking to build strength, compound exercises

such as bench presses,squats and dead-lifts would be used with very low rep counts 14
in the neighborhood of 3-5, with long rest periods of 3 minutes.

The speed at which you do reps in an exercise also results in very specific adaptations. If you want to increase your punching speed, you could try bench presses using heavy weights. Unfortunately, due to the heavy load used in the bench press, the movement would necessitate a slow speed. According to the SAID principle, lifting heavy weights slowly will result in an increased ability to lift heavy weights slowly and have minimal impact on movements like punching speed.

Building size and strength in most muscle groups requires sets of 6-10 reps with moderate-heavy poundages, while legs and forearms require higher reps due to their extended use during daily life. Studies have shown these to be the best parameters to achieve these goals.

If looking to gain as much size and strength as possible, we should be training all sets to failure and making use of a number of HIT variables. I have provided an explanation of many of the HIT variables but there are more available to use in your training. See my book, Dr. HIT's Effective High Intensity Variables, available at Amazon,Google, other online sellers and booksellers everywhere for an expanded list and step-by-step instructions on their use.

Focusing Effort On The Muscle Being Trained

There is a 'mind-muscle' link that can be developed with practice during your workout. Most upper body exercises utilize the arms during their performance. A great example is the lat pull-down. As you pull the handle down to your chest, you notice your biceps becoming fatigued. What will happen is your stronger lat muscles will outlast your weaker biceps muscles, preventing them from being exhausted before your biceps do. There are two methods for remedying this.

The first method is to pre-exhaust the lats by doing an isolation exercise before the lat pull-downs as outlined in the section on pre-exhaust. A great combination is a set of machine pullovers to exhaustion (isolation) followed by a set of lat pull-downs(compound.) The lats do most of the work during the lat isolation exercise while the biceps rest. During the pull-downs, the biceps, which are fresh, help force the lats past the point of typical failure.

The other strategy is to focus more of the effort on the lats while doing pull-downs by relaxing the biceps and concentrating the weight onto the lats while pulling the bar down. It seems simplistic but it works. Just keep practicing and you will become good at it. This works on all muscles, such as focusing effort off the triceps during the bench press, accenting the weight to the biceps and off the forearms during curls,etc.

The Need To Set Goals

With any other worthwhile endeavor, there is a need to track one's progress to determine if a given training regimen is working or not, or if enough effort is being put forth to produce the results you desire. The surefire way to do this is to set goals which are realistic to attain with hard work and proper rest. When beginning training, gains will come quickly. It's very easy to take for granted that gains will always come this rapidly, but that's not the case. In the beginning, set goals that are more aggressive in nature, such as gaining 10 lbs. of muscle in 6 months.

After you've been training for 12 months or longer, revise the goal to gaining a solid 10 lbs. of muscle per year. Another strategy which will lead to success is the addition of 2.5 lbs. per week to the poundage of each exercise. In a year's time the gain in strength and muscle size will be enormous. Take a look at the bench press. If 2.5 lbs. were added for an entire year, you would have a 130 lb. Increase!

Goals for fat loss and conditioning are great too. A realistic goal would be the loss of 2-3 lbs. of fat per week. That goal could be attained with a reduced carb/caloric eating revision in your diet as opposed to a dieting program, which almost surely would lead to failure as most diets lead to a net weight gain. Bottom line-make all goals attainable with hard work and specific. If you're vague, it will be hard to accurately measure your progress.

Some examples of good goal setting would be to aim to add 1/4” to your biceps measurement in three months or 2” on your chest measurement in three months. Of course, you want the size gained to be muscle not fat. So it is imperative that you keep an accurate measurement of your body-fat percentage or at least your waist measurement. If your arms are increasing in size but your waist is as well, chances are you're gaining fat at the same time-not good!

The Advantages Of Training With A Partner

Don't like training with a partner? You might want to reconsider after reading this. Working out with a partner during your training session gives you certain advantages not afforded the lone wolf trainee. Sure, it gives you the opportunity to tell your less-than-funny jokes to an unfortunate,committed victim. But all kidding aside,there are many valid reasons to call your buddy up and get going!

There are the obvious safety concerns like spotting squats and bench presses but there are other pluses as well. Those desiring increased intensity in their workouts will be able to have a helping hand assist them with completion of an extra rep or two to take a set

past failure. Pure negative training,where the barbell is lifted to the top by an 16
assistant and lowered by the bodybuilder is best accomplished with a helper or two. The give-and-take of ideas as to how to improve your form,strategies and goals proves to be invaluable. And don't forget the priceless advice you can give and get from your fellow fitness enthusiast.

Practical Overloading

Beginners experience dramatic size and strength increases in the initial phase of their training. This continues throughout the intermediate stages as a result of the "newness" of the exercise-induced stress. Soon the beginning bodybuilder turns into an intermediate one. The bodybuilding magazines espouse the latest training routine put forth by Mr. this and that champion, which sound appealing to the intermediate, and soon experienced bodybuilder so he continues to add sets and exercises to his routine and the results quickly diminish to a slow crawl after 12-24 months.

It's impossible to acquire unusual levels of strength and muscle growth by casually coaxing your muscles with lackluster workouts or by simply "confusing them" with constantly changing training routines. While it is advantageous to change your routine around and add new exercises while subtracting others, one of the most important factors to progress is the increase in the amount of weight, or load, they are being forced to contract against. This must take place during brief bouts of heavy effort. Muscle growth is a systemic response to an enormous overload having been imposed on the muscles via their contracting, whether concentrically, statically, eccentrically, or in combination, against a very heavy and demanding resistance.

Keep accurate training charts and make a note of rep counts, time under tension and weights used at each session. Attempt to add weight to the machine or barbell, even if its only 2-5 pounds. If a bodybuilder is willing to commit himself to training maximally and use progressive resistance in his workouts, the size and strength of his muscles will increase.

Micro-loading

One of the most important facets of building muscle and strength is the amount of resistance used and the strategy to increase the load used in a given exercise. If the load is jumped up too quickly, the nervous system will attempt to avoid injury by shutting down the ability to lift the weight using the Golgi Tendons. They are located at the insertion point of the tendons on the bones and protect the muscles and tendons from excessive force.

By increasing the weight incrementally, the Golgi Tendon reflex will be avoided,

resulting in successful load improvement. One of the best tools for doing this are
micro-loading plates. These weigh between 1 1/8-1 ¼ pounds each and can be attached
to a weight stack or placed on a barbell. There are magnetized add-on plates that weigh .
5,1,1 ½, 2 ¼ and 5 pounds each as well.

It is very important to attempt to increase the weight at each training session. Use a
weight that maxes you out at the desired rep count, say 8 reps. When you are able to do
10 reps, increase the weight by 2.5-5 pounds so you hit failure at 8 reps. Continue in this
cycle of adding weight and increasing reps at every workout.

Double Overloading

An expansion of the overloading principle, this method works by increasing the reps and
weight at the same time. Load a weight that allows 8 reps to failure. Attempt to increase
the weight by 2 ½ pounds and the rep count to 10 during the same set. If able to attain
this goal, increase the weight and reps at the next workout. You'll want to adjust the reps
back down every 2-3 workouts or the rep counts will get too high. It is possible to add
strength and muscle size quickly with this technique due to the quick increase in reps
and weight. Even though micro-loading using small weight increases seems like a slow
road to strength and muscle growth, think how much of an increase in strength 5 pounds
a week is at the one year mark!

The Science Of Muscle Growth

The accepted belief on stimulating muscle growth is that muscle growth is confined to
the muscle being trained. Actually, muscle growth is instigated by the central nervous
system in response to intense training efforts. This won't occur by the execution of low
intensity, repetitive work that fails to put a task on the body.

Attention must be paid to training the entire body, with strict attention to the large
muscles. Science has shown that when the legs are trained there is a general growth
stimulation to the entire musculature. Extra growth hormone and testosterone are
released which add to the growth response.

Many bodybuilders focus on compound exercises that target the chest, back and leg
muscles, while involving the smaller muscles of the body to attain maximum
hypertrophy. Heavy weights lifted for as many reps as possible, under strict control with
no extra momentum, within a specific time frame impose a maximum overload, not only
on the localized muscles but on the central nervous system.

It's important not to confuse increased strength and muscle mass as full repair and
recuperation of all bodily systems. These are merely adaptive responses and don't

reflect physiological health. The stress incurred by your central nervous system
each time you push yourself in an intense workout, even if adding only one plate on the
bar or one repetition to your all-time record. The amount of stress imposed on the body
daily and weekly accumulates over a lifetime.

Arthur Jones, the inventor of Nautilus Strength Machines, stated, "It is only rational to
use that which exists in limited supply as economically as possible." Because our
bodies can only supply a very limited supply of energy throughout our lifetimes, it only
makes sense that exercise be as brief as possible so as not to cause over-training.

The body must receive greater stress to continue progressing or your training will lag
and yield little or no results. Traditional high volume training is leads to an initial round
of gains but this eventually slows down as it depletes the body of energy and leads to
over-training. Bodybuilders need to increase the intensity of training through progressive
overload and application of the HIT techniques listed in this book and my other books
on HIT training.

Put forth as close to 100% effort into a limited training volume until you feel confident
that no additional effort was possible. If necessary, enlist the aide of an experienced high
intensity training coach to guide you to the proper level of intensity and effort. Train as
hard as you possibly can then go home and rest.

Enough recovery time must occur before resuming training. Growth stimulation happens
during training; muscle growth and strength increases during rest. If a muscle is still
sore from the previous session wait a few days before attempting to train that muscle
again. Try going to the gym and doing a few light "non-working" sets to flush blood into
the muscle. This brings valuable nutrients into the muscle , which aides the muscle in it's
rebuilding. If soreness continues for more than a week or two, it will be necessary to
reevaluate thee level of intensity, volume, and frequency.

Allow a few days between workouts, even if you are training different muscles than the
previous session. A point to keep in mind is the energy drain the large muscles of the
body enact upon the central nervous system. Legs, chest and back muscles are the
largest in the body-and while they are great for the stimulation of overall growth-cause a
large energy drain. Recovering from a hard leg workout the day after a hard chest one
can lead to over-training if intense back-to-back sessions occur on a regular basis. The
amount of recuperation necessary will largely depend on the intensity of effort and total
volume of each training session.

Avoiding Over-training

It is imperative to prevent over-training if you want to continue to achieve steady gains

without extreme fatigue, constant illness and general rundown. Here are some ways   19
to do this:
Develop a logical training system using the recommendations outlined throughout this
volume and my other books. Avoid excessive training volume as this can prevent your
muscles from recuperating from exercise-induced stress. Train using brief, intense
workouts with adequate rest. Too much stress in one area, such as home life or work, can
effect your training. Make sure to get at least 7-8 hours of sleep a night.

Short periods of rest and relaxation help to replenish the body and mind for future
physical activity. Use layoffs as an important part of your training, as they allow
complete recuperation from the intense , regular training HIT bodybuilders engage in.
Remember,there is a difference between being lazy and actually using a rest period
because of mental or physical fatigue, so be careful not to get out of the habit of regular,
healthy, intense exercise.

Bodybuilders normally train too often, thinking their muscle size will evaporate if they
aren't training every day. What makes this worse is the erroneous advice received from
bodybuilding magazines. The bodybuilders featured in these magazines, most of which
are chemically-enhanced, recommend routines that lead to severe over-training. The
inventor of Nautilus strength machines, Arthur Jones, was the first to declare the '96-
hour rule' back in the 1970s. He stated that muscle loss occurs within 96 hours if no
training takes place. Even though he later revised his statement , the '96 hour rule' is still
followed in many circles to this day.

Bodybuilders recuperate at different levels, and many need more rest than the typical
HIT rule of thumb of training each muscle once every 7-10 days. It will be necessary to
experiment with frequency of training until you reach your ideal, individualized
program. Begin by training each muscle every 7 days. At the second workout take notice
if your strength and zeal for training has decreased from the initial session. If so, rest
your muscle 10 days prior to resuming training. If still not fully-recovered, increase the
rest period to 14 days before training the muscle again.

Failure To Improve When Over-training Is Not The Culprit

If you haven't been making the progress you feel you should be and have determined
that over-training isn't the culprit, there are a number of other reasons for the lack of
results you've been experiencing. They are:

Age (can no longer improve; focus on maintenance or slow regression)
Genetics (reached a peak; can no longer improve in muscle size or strength)
Over-adaptation (mentally bored; lack of motivation; physically adapted to stimulus)
Previous Demands (each set performed diminishes subsequent workout capacity)

Insufficient Demands (lack of stimulus -i.e., intensity, sets, or frequency to cause a
sufficient alarm reaction.)

Pay attention to what your body tells you and keep a realistic set of goals. It could be that you have attained all of the muscle size and strength your body is capable of.

Wrong Selection of Training Routines

Many of us attempt to follow top champion bodybuilders' routines because we feel since they have achieved much success in the sport by training using these routines we should use them too. The truth of the matter is many of these routines are not what the bodybuilder is actually using. They appear in articles meant to impress the reader with the bodybuilder and to further his career.

These bodybuilders are using chemical-enhancement, that is steroids, human growth hormone, insulin and other anabolic drugs. These drugs allow the champion to over train on a regular basis because they increase the body's recuperative abilities and cause positive nitrogen balance, causing the muscles to rapidly grow.

Unfortunately they also lead to many health problems such as heart disease, kidney failure and cancer, to name a few. The ideal training routine is one which is designed around the present conditioning, the recuperative abilities and the goals of the bodybuilder. Remember to design it around the intensity principle outlined above.

Sample Variable Intensity Program For Arms
Phase 1

The first phase is similar to what is done by beginning bodybuilders. Emphasis is placed on form and the learning of proper exercise technique instead of heavy, intense training. Complete the desired exercises using good form, stopping the set two reps before hitting failure (the point where no more reps are possible).

Barbell curls-1x10
concentration curls-1x12
seated palms-facing pull-downs-1x12
standing triceps push-downs-1x12
standing triceps kickbacks-1x12
standing bar dips-1x12

Phase 2

The second phase increases the intensity of effort by ending all sets one rep before

failure. We will keep the set count at three each.
machine curls-1x10
seated incline curls-1x12
seated palms-facing pull-downs-1x10
lying triceps extensions-1x10
seated triceps overhead extensions-1x12
close-grip bench presses-1x12

Phase 3

The third phase is where we take all sets to the point of muscular failure. Load the bar or weight machine with a weight that causes you to put all-out effort to complete the desired amount of reps. Don't stop when you hit your rep count; attempt to grind out more reps. This causes you to overload your muscles and add weight every workout which will lead to additional muscle growth. Since we are increasing the level of intensity we will be reducing the set volume to two sets for both muscles.

concentration curls-1x12
bent over palms-facing barbell rows-1x10
angled-forward cable triceps extensions-1x12
seated machine triceps dips-1x8

Now that I've outlined all three phases of this HIT periodization schedule, begin to use it in your training by working with each phase for 3 weeks before progressing to the next level.

The Need To Use Both Power And Isolation Exercises

I am a strong advocate of the use of both free weights and machines to build muscle. There are some misconceptions circulating in the fitness and bodybuilding world that free weights are the only valuable tool when it comes to adding power and size. That's simply not true! Barbells and dumbbells are versatile and have many different exercises available to use with them. But weight machines offer unique training tools to a bodybuilder's program.

It's true weight machines have a more limited number of exercises available, but have their own advantages such as ease of use, ability to focus resistance more effectively on the muscle due to the elimination of the need to balance weight and an improved strength curve.

A great example of the advantages of machines over free weights is the barbell curl compared to the machine curl. When you begin the barbell curl the weight seems to get heavier and peaks at the mid-point, which is usually where the sticking point is. As you muscle it past this point, the resistance decreases until it is mostly non-existent at the top. In comparison, a properly cammed machine with an ideal strength curve, will begin with a heavy resistance and continue to provide this throughout the movement until it peaks at the end. This peaking is the best way to activate a large number of fibers in the muscle.

To train biceps muscles, I like to use both power exercises like palms-forward barbell rows and isolation exercises such as concentration and preacher curls. This allows complete exhaustion of the biceps and the addition of assistance muscles like the back muscles to help push the biceps past the point of muscular failure with the use of such HIT techniques like Pre-exhaust super-sets.

Straight Set Routines-Isolation

Routine #1
- Barbell preacher curls-1x10+ 4 forced reps
- zero rest
- Standing cable curls-1x10+burn reps at end of set

Routine #2
- Lying flat dumbbell curls-1x12+ 1 static hold at top (10-second)
- zero rest
- Dumbbell hammer curls-1x8+4 negative reps at end of set (cheat the dumbbells up and lower to an 8 count.)

Pre-exhaust Bicep Routines

The following routines make use of fresh, back muscles to "push" the biceps , which have been exhausted by isolation exercises to work them past the point of muscular failure. These routines are a great example of brief, intense, HIT routines, designed to build maximum muscle in minimum time.

Routine #1-Isolation+Compound

Dumbbell concentration curls-1x8+3 forced reps at end of set
zero rest
Seated palms-facing chin-ups (use a dip belt to add weight as necessary)-1x8+4 negatives at the end of set

Take all sets to muscular exhaustion or the benefit will be greatly reduced. Rep cadence should be 2/4.

Routine #2-Isolation+Compound

Incline dumbbell curls-1x10+ 3 static holds at end of set (hold the dumbbells for 10 seconds at the bottom,mid-point and top of the range of motion.
zero rest
Palms-forward barbell rows-1x6+3 negatives at end of set (Partner assists in raising the bar up and lower to a count of 8.)

If pre-exhaust super-sets are done correctly, low set counts will be ideal and very effective at building strength and size. It is extremely important to move from one exercise to the next because your muscles recoup 50% of their strength in as little as three seconds.

Power Biceps Routine

Always strive to add weight to the bar or machine at every workout in order to add muscle and strength. Typically, strength precedes size increases.

Barbell curls-1x6-8+ 2 cheat reps at end of set
20 seconds rest
Barbell drag curls-1x8+ 3 negatives at end of set

Frequency of Bicep Training

Now that I've given you a number of routines to use in your HIT training, I'll outline how often to train and combine the routines into a complete training program to develop huge biceps.

Week one
Train biceps 1x/week- Pre-exhaust routine

Week two
Train biceps 1x/wk- power routine

Week three
Train biceps 1x/wk- Giant set routine

Week four
Train biceps 1x/wk- Straight set routine

Maximizing Aerobic Potential by Arthur Jones

Owner/Founder -Nautilus and Med-ex Strength Equipment

Most of the scientists who have been involved in the field of exercise physiology during the last thirty years have devoted the vast majority of their attention to research related to the results of aerobic exercises, exercises performed for the purpose of improving cardiovascular condition.

Very similar exercise and testing procedures have been performed literally thousands of times in hundreds of schools all over this country, and the supposedly scientific journals have devoted most of their attention to such studies.

Why? Primarily, I believe, because the people who performed all of this research were attempting to limit their efforts to things that they could measure, attempts to determine the direction and magnitude of any physiological changes that resulted from such exercises. Improvements in cardiovascular condition certainly have value, but, in general, the most commonly used exercises that have been utilized in attempts to produce such cardiovascular improvement also produce physiological changes that are not desirable; if you are attempting to increase your muscular size or strength, or both, then you should avoid most of the aerobic exercises that are now being used like the plague,* because, almost inevitably, they will lead to over-training for your muscles, on the one hand not being hard enough to stimulate muscular growth, and on the other hand overworking your muscles to such a degree that overuse atrophy, a loss of muscular size and strength, will result.

If there is a successful bodybuilder in the world who ever performed much, if literally any, aerobic exercise then he has not come to my attention; yet it does follow that such people have poor cardiovascular ability; in fact, many of them have far better cardiovascular ability then the level shown by a typical hardcore jogger.

Having preached the gospel that "more is better," that if running fifty miles a week is good then running two-hundred miles a week is better, for nearly thirty years, even the "Father of aerobic exercise," Dr. Kenneth Cooper finally seems to be coming to his senses.

But, then, like most fanatics, having gone overboard in one direction initially, Cooper now appears to have gone overboard in another direction. Fairly recently, Cooper said, or words to that effect, that people who perform more than one hour of exercise weekly are not doing it for physiological reasons; but, even more recently, he has started to believe that exercise may cause cancer if overdone.

Personally, knowing him quite well, I would suggest that Cooper concern himself with things that he understands, which might limit him to things like tying his own shoes, if he is ever capable of that.

Almost since day one, and still very much in evidence almost anywhere you look, there has been an almost universally accepted myth about exercise that might be best described as an "either/or" belief; in effect, you must train "this way" for increasing muscular size and strength and "that way" for improving cardiovascular condition, must lift weights to build strength and must jog to increase cardiovascular condition.

Half of which belief is true, since jogging will do very little or nothing to build strength and will, in fact, if overdone, as it usually is, do quite a bit in the way of reducing both muscular size and strength. But it is not true that proper strength-building exercise will do nothing for cardiovascular condition.

Properly performed, which they seldom are, strength building exercises are not a "good" way to improve cardiovascular condition, they are, instead, by far the best way to improve cardiovascular condition. Strength building exercises require a level of resistance that is high enough to lead to momentary muscular failure after a few repetitions while exercises for improving cardiovascular condition involve a very low level of resistance which will not lead to muscular failure after a few repetitions. Anaerobic (heavy) exercise or aerobic (light) exercise.

If, as usually happens, you perform a set of heavy exercise for strength building purposes, and then sit on your ass or shoot the shit with a friend for five minutes before performing the next exercise, then you probably will increase both your muscular size and strength, will doing little or nothing in the way of improving your cardiovascular condition.

But if, instead, you move almost immediately from the end of the first exercise to the start of the second exercise, with almost no rest between the two exercises, then you will increase both strength and cardiovascular condition; in fact, that style of training, properly performed, will lead to a level of cardiovascular condition that is far higher than you could ever produce by any amount of jogging or any other cardiovascular exercise. Such a style of exercise simultaneously provides anaerobic exercise for strength building and aerobic exercise for improving cardiovascular condition.

BUT, A STRONG WORD OF CAUTION: do not jump feet first into such a style of training with no preparation; doing so without a careful period of preparation will, at best, make you as sick as a poisoned dog, and might literally kill you. So devote at least two weeks, and maybe as much as four weeks, to a gradual "break in" to such training;

start with a three minute rest between exercises, and then gradually reduce the rest periods until you are moving from one exercise to the next as fast as possible. Once you reach the target rate of exercise you will find that your pulse rate remains at a very high rate throughout the workout, far higher than you could ever maintain with any sort of aerobic exercise; yet your muscles are being worked anaerobically, as they must for strength-building purposes.

This is not an "easy" style of exercise nor is it "pain free," but it will produce very good results that can be produced in no other fashion. We used this style of training during research conducted at the United States Military Academy, West Point, twenty-two years ago, and the results were so outstanding that Dr. Kenneth Cooper refused to believe them, refused even though his own people performed all of the pre and post testing. Average strength for the test group increased by 60 percent in six weeks, while their cardiovascular condition reached a level so high that Cooper refused to believe it, a level he could not reach in six years of aerobic exercise.

When we first started using this style of training, in 1970, we quickly learned two things about it: ONE, such training must be started gradually, as mentioned above, and if not then it will literally make people sick, immediately sick, sick to the point of vomiting and then passing out.

TWO, even after such training is being performed, following the essential "break in" period outlined above, producing the best possible results requires such a style of training no more than once a week. During the research at West Point, we trained the cadet subjects three times each week but used this "no rest" style of training only once each week.

Prior to the West Point research, we had been working on the development of strength-testing tools for more than three years, but no such tools were available to us for testing purposes, the prototype testing tools that we did have simply did not work. So evaluating the increases in strength that were produced required us to judge these strength increases by comparing the starting level of resistance and number of repetitions performed to the same two factors at the end of the training period for six weeks; which requirement, unavoidable, introduced some unknown degree of error; nevertheless, the strength increases were so dramatic that any unknown degree of error in the testing procedures were relatively unimportant.

Basing their results upon almost identical testing procedures, most of the literally hundreds of research projects that have been conducted and reported by scientists all over the world during the last thirty years the published results have usually indicated strength increases of about 20 percent following 12 weeks of exercise using 9 sets of each exercise during each week of the training period. In contrast, we produced 60 percent strength increases, three times as much as those reported by most other people, and these results were produced in only 6 weeks of training rather than 12 weeks, so our "elapsed time" was only half as long as usual, and, finally, our results were produced by only 3 sets of each exercise weekly rather than the usual 9 sets of each exercise, which means that our weekly exercise was only a third of the usual training schedule.

So our overall, six-week program consisted of a total of only 18 sets of each exercise, rather than the usual total of 108 sets used by other researchers, yet our results were three times as good as theirs were; and, of course, our program produced literally enormous improvements in cardiovascular condition while the other programs, conducted in a usual manner with a lot of rest between exercises, produced little or nothing in the way of cardiovascular improvements.

A detailed report of this research program was published in The Athletic Journal in 1975, and has been ignored by almost everybody ever since.
And it should be noted that all of the pre and post ("before" and "after") testing was conducted, in the case of cardiovascular results, by doctors from Dr. Kenneth Cooper's Aerobic Institute in Dallas, and, in the case of strength increases, by doctors on the staff of West Point; neither I nor anybody associated with me had anything to do with the testing, this being a requirement imposed by me in an attempt to avoid a later charge that the published results had been overstated.

And just what, you might ask, did anybody in the scientific community learn from this study? Not a damned thing, of course, what would you expect? What few, if any, scientists who even bothered to read it apparently either did not believe it or failed to understand the significance of the results. And remember: these are the same people who, in general, swallow the lies published by Cybex hook, line and sinker.

During that research at West Point all of the cadet subjects were closely supervised during every exercise in order to make sure that the exercises were performed properly and in order to provide us with accurate records of their progress from workout to workout. Conducting research in that manner is both very time-consuming and very expensive; my total costs related to that study were in excess of $1,000,000.00, a large part of which expenses resulted from the fact that the entire program was recorded on 16mm professional motion-picture film that was filmed using more than a dozen professional cameras.

Altogether, we used more than 500,000 feet of film. All of these cameras being synchronous, meaning that the film was exposed at an exact rate of 24 frames per second, thereby providing us an exact record of the time involved in each exercise, speed-of-movement used during the exercise as well as elapsed time.

Nobody else in the history of the world ever came anywhere close to conducting research with such precision, or devoted so much time and money to their research. Years later, after the only testing tools capable of conducting meaningful and accurate testing of muscular strength were available to us, the MedX machines, we invested many millions of dollars in research with tens-of-thousands of subjects.

Altogether, more than sixty such research programs have now been conducted, and many of these studies have been published in several scientific journals; yet, in general, they are still being ignored by the scientific community.

If and when the scientific community ever comes to its senses, which I doubt, they could learn a lot of things that they need to know but do not now even suspect.

*I don't agree with this statement. Aerobic training , done in the proper dosage is very important for one's health.

Standard High Intensity (HIT) Techniques
Failure Training

Many bodybuilders use weight loads that allow them to complete the desired number of reps before reaching muscular failure, where no more full reps are able to be completed. While this stresses the muscle, it fails to provide the necessary stimulus to involve the maximum number of muscle fibers. HIT bodybuilders almost always end their training sets after reaching failure in an effort to maximize muscular stimulation. Taking a set to failure means ending the set when no more full reps are possible while exerting yourself nearly 100% in an attempt to perform one more rep.

Remember, a muscle doesn't keep track of the number of sets that you do, it needs just the right amount of stimulation to grow-no more -no less. If a bodybuilder intends on doing a certain number of sets of an exercise-say 10 sets of barbell curls, it would be necessary to pace his or her workout to allow completion of the specified number of sets. All but the 10th set would be sub-maximal and mostly useless for muscle growth.

Cheat Reps

In HIT training we stress slow, steady rep execution to put stress on the muscle, while minimizing the risk of injury. This prevents momentum in an exercise from subjecting tendons and ligaments to ten times the normal pressure they would experience during a typical intensity set. However, there are times when we can loosen the form of our reps to allow either more weight to be used during the concentric, or lifting portion or to do a set of negatives while training alone in certain exercises.

To demonstrate this, select load a barbell with a weight that causes failure at 8 reps, but instead of ending the set there, cheat the bar up to the top carefully with a hip swing and lower slowly to a count of 8. Repeat for 4 negative reps. This is one of the only ways to do negatives when training alone.

Another way to use cheat reps is to complete a set of 8 reps in the barbell curl, then use enough cheating force to allow completion of extra reps. This form of cheat reps is very similar to forced reps except for the momentum and extra speed involved, so while it is an effective technique, it is not a replacement for them.

How To Make Effective Use Of Super-sets

Super-sets are a great way of condensing a lot of work into a shortened time frame. They increase intensity as a result and can take many forms. Two exercises for the same muscle can be done back-back or a pair of exercises can be done for antagonistic muscles,i.e. biceps and triceps. A Giant set is 4-6 exercises done consecutively, with no rest, that are for either the same muscle group or antagonist muscles.

Pre-exhaust Super-sets

This form of super-set uses an isolation exercises to exhaust the target muscle followed by a compound one to train it past the point of normal failure. There is no need to have the assistance of a training partner, so this form of HIT is convenient to use.

A great example of this technique is the leg extension/leg press super-set. If you perform leg extensions first to failure, the quads will be exhausted. Without rest, complete a set of leg presses to failure. Use a slow rep speed, as with typical HIT training of 2/4. This eliminates any momentum, preventing injuries and keeps the load on the muscles throughout the exercise.

Leg extensions use fresh hip and other muscles to push the frontal leg muscles past failure-making this a very productive super-set. Other great combinations are: Pek dek flyes/Machine bench press, Dumbbell pullovers/Lat pull-downs and Dumbbell front raises/Barbell press.

It is very important to complete both exercises with no rest in-between them or you will lose most of the benefit. If you rest as little as three seconds the muscle will recuperate 50%. We want to completely exhaust the muscle, so please avoid this.

Back

Nautilus pullovers-1x15
zero rest
Machine rows-1x8

Chest

Pek dek flyes-1x12
zero rest
Machine bench press-1x6

Shoulders

Side delt raises-1x15
zero rest
Dumbbell presses-1x8

Legs-Quads

Leg extensions-1x15
zero rest
Leg press-1x12

Legs-Hamstrings

Leg curls-1x12
zero rest
Stiff-legged dead-lift-1x12

Biceps

Barbell preacher curl-1x12
zero rest
Palms-facing pull-downs-1x10

Triceps

Standing cable power push-downs-1x10
zero rest
Close-grip barbell bench press-1x10

Double pre-exhaust

This is similar to regular pre-exhaust with the exception two isolation exercises are done prior to one compound exercise. This provides greater in-roading of the target muscle due to the muscle being thoroughly exhausted prior to the compound movement.

Here is a great workout using this technique. Feel free to substitute exercises for variety.

Pek flyes on pek dek-1x15
Decline dumbbell flyes-1x12
Machine bench press-1x6

As in the standard pre-exhaust routine, you may utilize forced reps to increase intensity. The following is an example:

Mid-pulley cable flyes-1x12
Decline dumbbell flyes-1x10
Incline dumbbell bench press-1x10+4 forced reps

Forced Reps

After reaching failure at the end of a set, a trainee is able to extend a set past normal failure by adding forced reps. Here's how you do it: go to failure on a set and have your training partner provide just enough assistance to allow you to complete 1-3 additional reps. The movement should be smooth and your assistant should only add enough force as is necessary.

Forced reps are the easiest form of HIT variable and are simple to understand the concept of why they are so effective. A large number of a muscle's fibers are activated during a failure set but not all fibers are exhausted completely. The forced rep causes the extension of a set, allowing the additional fibers to be completely fatigued.

Negative Reps

These can be done at the end of a set for additional muscle in-roading or exclusively. To do them at the end of a set, go to failure then have an assistant lift the bar or machine for you and transfer the weight to you in a smooth motion. Lower the weight and repeat for the desired number of negatives. To do a negative-only set, load the bar or machine with 140% of the weight you normally use. Have an assistant lift the bar or machine arm to the top then shift the weight to you. Lower to an eight count. Repeat.

You'll notice these will give you a deep soreness 1-2 days after training. This is due 32
to the higher-than-normal degree of micro-tears in the muscle fibers compared to typical
HIT training. These are very effective at building strength due to the extra load one is
able to use during negatives. When a heavy weight is lowered, the muscle's fibers create
a strong friction between themselves, which aids in it's ability to control extreme
poundages.

Forced Negative Reps

While negative reps are one of the most intense forms of training possible, they can be
made even more effective by having a training partner apply additional pressure on the
bar or machine's arms to make the weight heavier and harder to resist on the way down.
The movement must be steady-with no jerky movements or injury is possible.

Use loads in the range of 140% of your 1RM(1 rep max) as you do for regular negatives.
Have your assistant raise the weight for you , or at least provide most of the effort. Fight
the downward descent of the bar while your assistant presses steadily down on the bar
with both hands. The tempo should be a count of 8. Repeat for a total of 8 reps, which
should be the point where it becomes difficult to control the movement of the weight
and is no longer safe.

Drop Sets

An efficient way to dramatically increase intensity quickly is drop sets. Use a weight
that causes muscular failure at the desired rep count. Quickly reduce the weight by one
plate on a machine or barbell and do a second mini-set to failure. Continue this way until
you have completed a total of 6-8 mini-sets. Selectorized machines are the best tool for
this form of training due to the ease of changing weight quickly. Fixed dumbbells and
barbells are also handy because of ease of use.

Drop sets allow as many as eight episodes of muscular failure in a single set. This ramps
up intensity and the recruitment of a large number of a muscle's fibers. The body has no
other option but to overcompensate by increasing muscle size/strength. They're similar
to forced reps in that they allow you to train past the point of muscular failure.

With forced reps, an assistant applies just enough pressure on the barbell, dumbbell or
machine arm to enable completion of additional reps after you reach failure. With drop
sets, after you reach failure you decrease the weight and continue until failing again.
This is continued until a series of failures occur. If a training partner isn't available this
technique is a great method to up the intensity of your workouts.

Rest-Pause

One of the problems with standard HIT training,or other types of training for that matter, is the buildup of lactic acid in the muscle from training. It leads to a strong burning sensation and possible cessation of a set. One of the ways to circumvent this problem is to allow the lactic acid to be flushed out of the muscle between reps during a set. Rest-Pause is one of the best ways to accomplish this.

This is done by doing a one-rep max followed by a 10-second rest period. A series of single reps are done in this fashion until the set is completed. Usually eight reps is sufficient to reach the proper in-roading of the muscle being trained. After the first or second rep, it will be necessary to reduce the poundage by 25-30% to allow completion of the rep. Continue reducing the weight enough to allow completion of the rep with as near 100% effort as possible.

You can use 3-reps in the same way. Use a weight that allows completion of three reps using max effort then rest ten seconds before doing the next 3-rep combo. Continue in the same way as above. Other low rep counts can be used as well with similar effectiveness. The main thing to focus on is the use of maximum poundages while using good form with no momentum to ensure a very high level of intensity.

This technique is great for building both strength and muscle growth because of the use of maximum poundages to push the limit of a muscle's capability and the brief 10-second rest, which flushes the lactic acid out of the muscle, as mentioned above. Many bodybuilders,though seasoned with years of training under their belt,have made incredible gains in size and strength in a short period of time with this method.

Infitonic Reps

Similar to Rest-pause training, in that it uses maximum effort singles separated by 10-second rest periods, this form of HIT adds forced negatives at the end of each rep. Intensity levels are increased dramatically by the additional stress to the muscle by the downward pressure of the forced negative. To put this into practice, select a weight that is your 1RM in the seated shoulder press machine and press it up. Your partner then presses down on the machine's handles with a firm downward pressure while you resist to a count of 8. The motion must be smooth with no jerkiness or you risk straining your muscle or tendons. This is called a forced negative contraction and adds new resistance to an already taxing procedure(negative rep.)

Omni-Contraction

An offshoot of rest-pause training, Omni-Contraction adds the additional component of static holds during the negative phase to increase the intensity level. The positive zone of rest-pause places maximum stress on a muscle's fibers while the static holds during the negative phase activate additional fibers to cause extra micro-damage and more overcompensation of the muscle by the body. The intensity level is very high and has to be experienced to fully appreciate it.

To use this technique with bench presses,lower the bar one third of the way and hold for 10 seconds. Lower to mid-point and hold for an additional 10 seconds. Lower to three inches off your chest and hold a final 10 seconds before lowering to your chest and pressing the bar up to the pre-lockout position. Rest 10 seconds then repeat. Like rest-pause, it will be necessary to reduce the poundages to allow completion of max , single reps.

Use a smooth motion throughout, avoiding jerky movements or excessive momentum to keep tension on the muscle(s) being trained. Enough weight should be used to cause maximum exertion on the positive portion of the rep and the static holds. You should attempt to reverse the downward movement of the resistance during the static holds.

Up and Down Set

This is an excellent variable to wear down a muscle as it recruits a large number of muscle fibers due to the fast pace and constant bombardment with one mini-set after another. The extra blood pump helps to stimulate muscle growth by increasing hydro-static pressure in the muscle. Since the pace is very fast, you'll get a lot of work done in a minimum amount of time, which really builds endurance and cardio conditioning.

Begin with a moderate resistance and perform 8 repetitions in the dumbbell overhead press. With less than 5 seconds rest, move up to the next heaviest load (a plate on a machine, the next heaviest set of dumbbells, or additional plates on a barbell if using those pieces of equipment). Do an additional 8 repetitions. Continue until you reach muscular failure with the heaviest weight possible. This concludes the upward portion of the set. Immediately decrease the load to the next lightest resistance.

Continue until reaching muscular failure, repeat. Keep going until you end at the weight with which you began. This series of events constitutes the down phase of the set. The total number of mini-sets should not exceed 5 on the up phase. If you can complete more than 8 reps before reaching a point of muscular failure during the fifth mini-set, increase the starting weight.

Static Holds

Standard high intensity training entails doing a set to failure, and possibly adding a   35
HIT variable or two, such as forced reps,forced negatives and the like. This allows HIT
bodybuilders to train their muscles with maximum intensity to foster new muscle
growth. It has been shown in medical studies that extreme intensity levels on a muscle
are quickly adapted to by the body, making them less effective
in our training.

Is it possible to increase intensity even further? The answer is yes. By reducing
movement during a set to near zero, maximum weights can be used,while avoiding the
limiting constraints like lactic acid buildup. Not only that but the chance of injury is
reduced drastically due to the elimination of momentum to complete reps during a set.
How exactly do you train with zero,or near zero movement during a set?

Static holds, or static contraction training, is a revolutionary method that uses extremely
heavy resistance held motionless in a fixed position for a pre-determined number of
seconds. As the bodybuilder progresses, the weight is held for a longer period of time.
Once the hold reaches a hold time at the top of the range desired, the weight is increased
and the hold time reverts back to the beginning one.

These are a great way to up the intensity in your workouts. In most cases, heavy
weights are used and the holds are usually 5-20 seconds in length. While training
partners aren't necessary, they make it easier to complete this technique.

There are many variations to this technique-we will be using a couple of them in this
book. While barbells and dumbbells are great tools to use, machines lend themselves to
this variable. There are several reasons for this. Machines use weight stacks, therefore its
impossible to drop heavy weights on yourself. Since resistance is changed with a pin,
weight changes are very fast. Machines' movement arms move in a controlled path so
there is no need to balance a weight like there is with free weights.

To demonstrate this technique, select a weight on the stack of a bicep curl machine that
allows you to hold the machine's arms for 10 seconds before the arms descend. Reduce
the weight one plate and repeat after a 10-second rest. Continue until six holds have
been completed. The handles should be held at the point of maximum contraction,
toward the top of the range of motion.

A sample workout looks like this:

Machine curls-1x6 holds,10-second holds,10-second rest periods in-between holds
Palms-up machine rows-1x6 holds,10-second holds,10-second rest periods in-between
holds

This workout takes advantage of the powerful effects of static holds and pre-exhaust.
The isolation exercise,machine curls exhausts the biceps and the compound movement, palms-up rows, finishes the biceps off.

Use maximum weights on all holds; the handles should begin to descend after 10 seconds due to muscular failure.

Static holds - during triceps press-downs on a cable machine

This system gives bodybuilders a perfect way to train all muscle groups safely. It has been criticized for being dangerous because of the use of heavy weights but is in fact very safe if good form is used and proper exercise performance is followed.

Suggested Training Routines:

Legs

Leg press-1x8 -10-second holds-hold just before lockout
Leg curl-1x8 -10- second holds-hold at top of movement
Toe presses on leg press-1x8 -10-second holds-hold at extended position

Chest

Machine bench press-1x8-10-second holds-hold just before lockout

Back

Machine row-1x8-10-second holds-hold against chest

Shoulders

Machine press-1x8-10-second holds-hold just before lockout 37

Biceps

Machine preacher curl-1x8-10-second holds-hold at fully curled position

Triceps

Seated machine triceps extensions-1x8-10-second holds-hold just before lockout

Static Hold Pyramid

An offshoot of static holds, pyramid static holds allow the trainee to use lighter weights than is often used while training using static holds. Trainees start with a sub-maximum weight and quickly build up to a maximum weight before descending down the stack. As with other static hold protocols, selectorized weight machines are the best tool choice to use due to their safety and ease of weight change.

We also use a different approach than with other static holds in that the trainee performs the holds by lifting the weights off the rest of the stack only about an inch and holds that in position for 20 seconds. Since this position is one of inferior strength for most muscles, it makes it possible to use lighter weights than we normally do in static hold training.

Using the incline bench press as an example, select a weight near your max and hold for 20 seconds. Rest 10 seconds and add another plate to the stack and hold for 20 seconds. Continue until a max weight is reached. Decrease the weight one plate at a time until you have worked your way down the stack. This technique can be used for all exercises, including isolation and compound movements and all muscle groups.

The 20-second count recruits an enormous amount of fibers and ensures momentary muscular failure without the use of the heavy weights used during typical static hold techniques. By using 20-second holds there will be effective loading and recruitment of fibers.
A sample workout for the chest using the incline bench press is as follows:

Incline bench press-1x10, 20-second holds

hold #1-80% of 1rm
hold#2-90% of 1 rm
hold#3-100% of 1rm
hold#4-90% of 1rm
hold#5-80% of 1rm

hold#6-70% of 1rm
hold#7-60% of 1rm
hold#8-50% of 1rm
hold#9-40% of 1rm
hold#10-30% of 1rm

As you can see, we worked our way up in weight by 10% on each successive hold and peaked in weight using maximum exertion before working our way back down in weight. This allowed us to use heavy weights while training with 100% exertion and avoiding risk of injury.

Once the first 20-second count is up the trainee slowly returns the resistance under control to the weight stack, whereupon the trainer immediately moves the pin down one notch on the weight stack and the trainee is once again instructed to "contract" his muscles against the resistance. This procedure is continued until load and fatigue combine to the point where the trainee either cannot lift the weight from the stack or cannot sustain his contraction against the resistance for the full 20-seconds.

At this point we reverse direction and — in the exact same fashion—proceed to have the trainee work his way back up the weight stack until he eventually returns to the load level he started with. These "contractions" (this series of static holds) can be likened to the "repetitions" of a conventional set, with each successive contraction, like each successive repetition, serving to recruit and fatigue out more and more motor units over the span of time of a conventional set until all available motor units (and motor unit types) have been recruited and fatigued out. A Max Pyramid set on the Leg Press, then, might look something like this:

1st contraction: 80 lbs x 20 seconds

2nd contraction: 90 lbs x 20 seconds

3rd contraction: 100 lbs x 20 seconds

4th contraction: 110 lbs x 20 seconds

5th contraction: 100 lbs x 20 seconds

6th contraction: 90 lbs x 20 seconds

Experienced trainees should limit their workout to two exercises, such as a Pull-down and Leg Press.

Allowing for the additional time required to raise and lower the weight (albeit only an inch or two) into position and the time required to pull out and reinsert the pin into a selectorized weight, the "Time Under Load" for this set might be in the neighborhood of 2 minutes and 40-seconds (give or take). The entire Time Under Load for a process such as this will vary depending, in my opinion, on the predominant fiber type that an individual possesses in the muscle group/s he or she is training (with trainees that are fast twitch dominant having a shorter TUL, and those that are slow twitch dominant having longer TULs).

After working his way back up the stack to his starting weight, the trainee will note that the same resistance that felt like nothing when he began the exercise now feels particularly challenging. And, after maxing out on his way down the stack, as he works his way back up and the weights get progressively lighter, the trainee will be able to more effectively control his contractions, thus keeping the load squarely on the targeted musculature as it progressively weakens.

The trainee's respiration will now be palpable as his cardiovascular system is in hyper drive in an attempt to process the lactic acid out of his muscles (which it does by back-engineering it to pyruvate and processing it through the aerobic system).

The distance the trainee moves the weight to begin the exercise is minimal, perhaps one-inch on an exercise such as the leg press. This places the muscle group being targeted in its worst possible leverage position, which means that muscular involvement will be at its highest since there are no structures other than muscular that are contributing to the movement or to the "holding" of the resistance. The distance the trainee will move his limbs to get to the position of maximum moment arm will vary depending upon the length of the involved levers (limb length) and the exercise he is performing. Since we typically only perform a "Big 3" or a variant thereof, here are the approximate "hold" points for these exercises:

1. Leg Press – approximately one inch off the stack.
2. Lat Pull-down – Upper arms should be 90-degrees to the body.
3. Overhead Press – approximately one-to-three inches off the stack.

The Leg Press and Overhead press are approximate, and will still require 40 the trainee to locate his own "sweet spot" where he feels his leverage to be the worst and the loading of his muscles the most. The Lat Pull-down can be made into an incredibly effective exercise that works almost every muscle in the upper body by incorporating the following six elements into its performance:

1. The torso should be at a 90-degree angle to the legs.
2. Draw the humerus down until it is 90-degrees from the torso (that's the hold point).
3. Hyper supinate the wrists so that your palms are facing East and West (or as close to that as you can).
4. Draw the elbows together until they touch in front of you while keeping your upper arms at a 90-degree angle
5. "Crunch" your abdominals by compressing your trunk downward (not by bending forward or by lowering your upper arms out of the 90-degree position).
6. Remember to "contract" into and out of the "Max Moment Arm" (again, for wont of a better term) position — don't think about "moving" or "lifting" weight, but rather "contracting" against the resistance.

What I personally like about this protocol is that, when you operate at a maximum moment arm or leverage disadvantage, any weight stack on any machine is more than adequate and the all of the available fibers that can be recruited get recruited in exactly the same way that they would if you were operating in a leveraged advantage position with heavier weights (as the leverage advantage simply requires more weight to be employed to overcome the involvement of the bones).

As Newton's 2nd Law states that when you push out with 200 pounds of force, 200 pounds of force pushes back at you, using progressively (and perhaps needlessly) heavier weights can create a growing "force" problem for trainees as they grow stronger. Fortunately, your muscles can't tell the difference; they only respond to force requirements. And by employing a leverage disadvantage that emphasizes maximum moment arm, you can effectively bring into play a sequential recruitment of motor units until all available motor units have been brought into service (from slow twitch through intermediate twitch to fast twitch).

And as maximum moment arm is the point where the targeted muscle group is maximally engaged, there exists no reason to compromise this stimulus by moving out of this position (hence the "hold" at this point). Again, the big advantage with this approach is that motor units are recruited and fatigued in a manner that dramatically minimizes the forces coming back to the body.

Chest press- Static Hold

Static Holds At The End Of A Set

Another great variation of static holds is to add a hold at the end of a failure set. Do a set of an exercise to failure then lift the bar or machine arm to the point of maximum contraction and hold for 10 seconds before returning. This activates a large number of a muscle's fibers after exhausting them during the main portion of the set, which is key to providing the ideal stimulus for new growth. Short pulsing reps,called burn reps,can be done just prior to the hold for an increased amount of muscle fiber recruitment. While it may be necessary to have the assistance of a partner to lift the weight into position for the hold, most of the time the weight can be lifted by the bodybuilder alone.

Usually the weight is held at the position of max contraction but I recommend changing hold positions frequently to maximize fiber usage during the set. Try holding at the midpoint of an exercise or the beginning and compare the level of contraction. Newer research has indicated that strength can be increased threefold in a short period of time by holding heavy weights in the pre-stretch position of an exercise.

There has been no complete explanation as to why this is so effective but try this with dumbbell preacher curls. Lower the weight all the way to the bottom, making sure to get a full stretch. Allow the weight to pull your arms down as far as is safe. Hold this for 20 seconds before resting for 10 seconds. Repeat with a lighter weight for another 20-second hold. This is great to use with pull-ups, overhead triceps dumbbell press, dumbbell bench presses and many other exercises.

The Revised Intensity Principle-The Proper Method To Vary The Intensity Level

The best way to work your way up the intensity ladder to build muscle is to begin with sub-failure resistance loads and increase efforts until maximum intensity levels have been reached then decrease levels by cycling back down in intensity. Realize that your best gains will be realized during periods of maximum intensity training as that is

the time when muscle stimulation will be greatest. The reason we are reducing the
intensity in the first place is to de-condition your muscles so they are no longer used to being pushed as hard as during normal HIT training. It won't take very long for them to become unaccustomed to intensity training and will respond positively once intensity training is resumed.

Stage One

- End sets two reps before failure

Stage Two

- End sets one rep before failure

Stage Three

- End sets at failure

Stage Four

- Add one or more HIT variables to one or more sets

Stage Five

- Add two HIT variables,performing one set per muscle group

This outline gives you a straight-forward method to cycle your training demands. It keeps your muscles guessing as it is in constant flux. My suggestion is to use steps three-five the majority of the time as they are the stages where you will be making real strength and muscle gains. The other ones are designed to de-load your muscles and sensitize them to high training intensity levels utilized in stages three-five. Two weeks in each stage should work well with the exception noted above.

A program for Chest training using full intensity variation is as follows:

Stage One

- Incline dumbbell flyes-1x12
- Decline dumbbell bench press-1x8
- Standing bar dips-1x10

- Pek dek flyes-1x15
- Push-ups-1x12
- Barbell bench press-1x6

Stage Three

- Decline dumbbell flyes-1x12

- Incline machine press-1x8

Stage Four

- Standing cable cross-over-1x15
- Seated machine dips-1x8+4 forced reps

Stage Five

- Incline machine press-1x8+ 4 forced reps+6 negative reps

Strong-Zone Partials and Other Partial Training

One of the initial rules you have drilled into your head when you start lifting weights is how important it is to use a full range of motion when training. You're told to train the entire muscle and avert developing imbalances that can decrease your flexibility and lead to injuries. This seems like sound advice, and is recommended for new bodybuilders, but if you've been training for a number of years, it is time to expand your training to a new level.

Many times bodybuilders are limited to using weight in an exercise that is the maximum they are able to handle in the weak zone, or sticking point. Take the bench press for example. The hardest point is the initial push off the chest. As the bar moves further, the triceps come into play and aid the chest in raising the weight. A heavier load could be used during the upper zone due to the higher involvement of the triceps, but its impossible to change the weight every rep midway through the press.

How do we overcome this? By loading the bar or machine with a weight that maxes you out at eight reps in the upper zone only and completing eight partials in the top zone only to failure. This overloads the chest, front delt and triceps muscles more effectively by the use of very heavy weights. Many so-called experts will tell you you need to always train using a full range in all of your exercises , but research has shown that not to be the case.

Training to failure in your strongest range of motion with much heavier weights is going to be much more intense than training to failure using a full range of motion. Because the load is heavier, a higher number of fibers are needed and activated to move the weight. Let's look at a male bodybuilder training using the barbell bench press.

If he is training with a weight on the bar of 250 lbs. for ten reps to failure, it stands to reason that he is limited to using that weight because that's all they are able to handle in the beginning of each rep, which is the point of the weakest zone. The fibers that are necessary to move the weight are recruited and no more. If he then loads the bar up to 350 lbs and has assistance in raising the bar, he will be able to do a series of reps in the top third zone. This will recruit a much higher number of fibers due to the heavier weight and increased intensity level.

I like to mix in strong-zone partials with standard sets because experience has shown this gives a thorough growth stimulation to the muscles. Begin with strong-zone partials first to maximize the amount of weight used then finish with another exercise done using other HIT techniques. Both isolation (barbell curls) and compound (palms-facing pull-ups) can be used for strong-zone partials, making them versatile. One workout use a compound movement and the next, an isolation exercise.

Attempt to add weight to the load every workout, using small increases in the neighborhood of 2-5 pounds, depending on the muscle being trained and the exercise. If too big of a jump in weight is used your nervous system will react by shutting down to avoid injury. This is the result of the Golgi Organ and is covered in one of my other books, so it won't be discussed in length.

Power-lifters often use maximum weights in their training primarily for a mental advantage, reasoning that if you become used to extremely heavy loads on your shoulders or in your hands, maximum lifting attempts won't feel nearly as daunting.

There is some suggestion that extremely heavy loads can alter the Golgi Tendon Organ, preventing muscular suppression under heavy loads.

Regardless of the reason for using extremely heavy weights, power-lifters often use reverse band lifts during their training. To set up reverse band lifts for squats, benches, or dead-lifts, simply attach the bands to the top of the power rack and to the bar. This causes you to handle most of the weight at the top of the lift, and as you squat down or lower the bar, the bands take progressively more of the load.

The end result is the use of heavier weights than you could normally handle 45 through a full range of motion because the bands make the load manageable through the most difficult part, or sticking point of the lift.

Superslow Training

Initially developed by Kenneth Hutchins, an associate of Nautilus inventor Arthur Jones, this technique dramatically slows down rep cadence to 10/4, 10-second positive, or lifting portion and 4-second lowering, or negative phase. Mr. Hutchins promoted his system as safer because the slower speed prevented trainees from using momentum to move the weight.

While that is true, the slower positive causes more tension in the muscle's fibers due to higher friction between the fibers which leads to more cross-bridging between fibers. These cross-bridges are the fibers sliding along each other to shorten or lengthen a muscle. The more cross-bridges per unit of time means greater tension created.

Training super slow can improve your overall strength due to higher muscle fiber recruitment and tension generated, according to Dr. Len Kravitz of the University of New Mexico. When you slow down the smallest filaments in your muscles, actin and myosin, form more cross-bridges during concentric and eccentric contraction. There is more micro-damage to the muscle as a result,which leads to greater growth. Some studies have shown a greater strength gain with this slower-speed training compared to standard-speed training.

Initially, the rep cadence was 10/10; a ten second positive and ten second negative. Through trial and error, it was determined that a ten second negative "allowed" the muscle to rest, which is unacceptable. The cadence which offers the best focus on the muscle while working the negative was determined to be 10/4. Due to the use of 14-second reps, it becomes necessary to reduce the rep count to 4 or 5 to keep the time under tension appropriate for the muscle being trained.

If we typically train our biceps with a tut of 60 seconds because of a mixed fiber makeup, using a rep cadence of 2/4 and 10 reps, we need to change the parameters to 10/4 with a rep count of 4 or 5 at most to keep in our range of 60-70 seconds.

Even though the proponents of Superslow training advocate using this technique to the exclusion of others, I have found the best practice is to cycle training between techniques. Use Superslow for several weeks before cycling in other forms of HIT training, otherwise your body quickly becomes acclimated to the stresses placed on it and ceases to respond. Feel free to cycle Superslow training into your workout program on a regular basis for great results.

To improve muscular endurance historically bodybuilders would typically perform an exercise for two to three sets of 12 or more repetitions. In super-slow training you use only one set, but that set can take up to three minutes depending on how many repetitions you perform. The longer you train the more you begin to see changes in local muscular endurance, in that the muscle gets better at doing the exercise for a longer period of time without fatigue. However, this does not translate to cardiovascular endurance, because the super slow method does not raise your heart rate enough to cause adaptation.

Super slow-motion training can be challenging because of the tension created in the muscles. Some people may find the challenge inspiring while others may be bored by the pace of the exercise.

Extended Slow Reps

In keeping with the spirit of HIT-taking things to the extreme-I introduce you to Extended Slow Reps. This builds on the benefits of super-slow reps-placing a high stress level on one's muscle fibers and increased cross-bridging of fibers- to increase the level of intensity further. Instead of utilizing a rep cadence of 10/4, we will be using one of 30/30. Yes, its excruciating to go that slow but don't worry the rep count will be restricted to 1-1.5 due to the necessity of keeping with the ideal time under tension (tut) to build new muscle growth.

If we were to keep reps in the same range as super-slow the tut would be excessive for growth and would alter our training away from muscle growth to endurance training. Since our rep tempo is 30/30, 30 seconds for positive, or concentric, and 30 seconds for the negative, or eccentric portion, rep count is 1-1.5 ,as noted above, for each exercise. There will be an extremely high number of muscle fibers recruited to do the job of lifting and lowering the weight because of the slow tempo.

On some exercises it is beneficial to begin with the negative. Others necessitate starting with the positive. Some examples of exercises to start with the negative are: barbell or machine presses,barbell or machine bench presses and barbell squats. Exercises that should begin with the positive include: barbell curls,chin-ups, pull-ups and lat pull-downs.

Initially, it will be tough to judge the amount of weight to use because of the distinct difference in execution to the typical HIT sets you have been doing. Once you begin using this technique you will soon develop an instinct about how much weight to use and the amount of weight to add to the bar or machine to micro-load yourself to a higher load in each workout.

It is a great idea to train with an experienced training partner who will be
able to observe your form and rep speed and assist with adding forced reps. In the
beginning when you're getting used to this technique and experimenting with load
levels, your partner will be able to give forced rep assistance to allow completion of the
rep. Even though free weights work great with this technique, machines offer a much
more controlled environment, which adds a large margin of safety and keeps you in the
proper movement path.

Extreme HIT (High Intensity) Routines

Failure training forms the nucleus of high intensity training. Studies have shown "going
to failure" on exercises, if done with enough effort, to be ideal for growth stimulation.
Following the previous recommendation of 2 sets(one set of two exercises) for most
muscles, like triceps, and 3 sets(one set of three exercises) for large ones like back, the
chance of over-training will be slim. More than one HIT variable can be used during a
set to maximize intensity and therefore, muscle growth stimulus.

Adding HIT variables, like the ones I've outlined, helps raise the intensity further by
forcing the muscles to work even harder and involving additional muscle fibers. These
workout sessions should be done on a rotating basis with failure ones to generate
maximum muscle growth potential, while preventing over-training.

There is a progression to these techniques with regard to the stress they place on the
muscles. Using a simple flow chart to demonstrate, a comparison would look like this:
**failure->super-slow reps-> forced reps->negative reps->rest-pause->infitonic-
>static holds->Omega set static holds**

While I didn't include all training protocols, this flowchart gives you a good outline as to
intensity levels of different variables. A good way to use this is to do a couple of failure
workouts and move up to the next level or two to increase intensity levels. Do a couple
of workouts at this level or add variety by substituting other techniques a level or two
above.

By adding additional variables into the mix, there's an almost infinite number of
techniques to choose from. This not only prevents boredom in your training, but enables
bodybuilders to build upon previous workouts to constantly find new ways to increase
muscle mass and strength.

To reduce training volume and increase intensity further, we will be using 2-3 different
HIT variables during each set of an exercise. This enables us to thoroughly train each
muscle using one set only. Due to the extreme intensity of this form of training, it will be
necessary to perform short cycles or risk severe over-training. In a two week cycle

do one workout using failure training, rest for 7-10 days, and complete an extreme 48
intensity one. HIT variables need to be properly grouped together or the performance of them will be both ineffective and awkward. If we were to group rest-pause with super-slow reps it would not only be awkward but the two forms of intensity training just don't go together by the nature of their execution. On the other hand, super-slow reps,forced reps and static holds go well together and will be used in our training. Get ready....we are about to turn up the intensity a notch-a big notch.

Chest Routines
Forced reps+Negatives+Static holds

Decline machine bench press-1x6+3/3/4
Performance:Use a weight that leads to failure at 6 reps. Have an assistant aid in the completion of 3 forced reps followed by 3 negative reps. Increase the weight slightly and have your assistant lift the weight into position for you at the point of maximum contraction, which is the ¾ mark in the decline bench press. It will be necessary to reduce the weight 10% on each successive hold due to muscle fatigue. Do a total of 4 static holds.

Extended slow reps+Negatives+ Superslow reps

Incline machine bench press-1x1/3/4
Performance:Use a weight that allows a max effort for one complete rep using a 30/30 rep cadence. Begin with the positive portion(concentric) before lowering. Increase the weight 20% and do 3 negative reps before reducing the weight, and using a rep cadence of 10/4, do a total of 4 super-slow reps to failure. The extended slow reps exhaust the chest muscles by activating a large number of fibers, the negatives take them past failure and the super-slow reps finish them off by subjecting them to elevated tension and increased fiber cross-bridging.

Rest-pause+Negatives+Static holds

Machine dips-1x3(6)/3/4
Performance:Use a weight that allows 3 reps to be completed. Reduce the weight by one plate and complete an additional 3 reps. Continue for a total of 6 cycles. Increase the weight by 30% , have an assistant lift the weight and transfer to you. Lower to an 8-count. Repeat for a total of 3 negatives. Do a series of 4, 10-second holds with a 10-second rest in-between.

Machine flyes-1x4/3/6
Performance: Use a weight that leads to failure at 4 reps using a rep cadence of 10/4.
Increase the weight and do 3 max holds for 10-seconds with a 10-second rest in-
between. Decrease the weight and do a series of 6 burn reps.

Back Routines
Forced reps+Negatives+Static holds

Machine rows-1x6+3/3/4
Performance:Use a weight that leads to failure at 6 reps. Have an assistant aid in the
completion of 3 forced reps followed by 3 negative reps. Increase the weight slightly
and have your assistant lift the weight into position for you at the point of maximum
contraction, which is the ¾ mark in the decline bench press. It will be necessary to
reduce the weight 10% on each successive hold due to muscle fatigue. Do a total of 4
static holds.

Extended slow reps+Negatives+ Superslow reps

Pull-ups-1x1/3/4
Performance:Use a weight that allows a max effort for one complete rep using a 30/30
rep cadence. Begin with the positive portion(concentric) before lowering. Increase the
weight 30% using a dip belt and do 3 negative reps before eliminating the weight, and
using a rep cadence of 10/4, do a total of 3 super-slow reps to failure. The extended slow
reps exhaust the back muscles by activating a large number of fibers, the negatives take
them past failure and the super-slow reps finish them off by subjecting them to elevated
tension and increased fiber cross-bridging.

Rest-pause+Negatives+Static holds

Machine rows-1x3(6)/3/4
Performance:Use a weight that allows 3 reps to be completed. Reduce the weight by one
plate and complete an additional 3 reps. Continue for a total of 6 cycles. Increase the
weight by 30% , have an assistant pull the handles forward and transfer them to you.
Lower to an 8-count. Repeat for a total of 3 negatives. Do a series of 4, 10-second holds
with a 10-second rest in-between.

Superslow+Static Holds+Burn reps

Machine pullovers-1x4/3/6
Performance: Use a weight that leads to failure at 4 reps using a rep cadence of 10/4.

Increase the weight and do 3 max holds for 10-seconds with a 10-second rest
in- between. Decrease the weight and do a series of 6 burn reps. Attempt to relax your grip on the machine's arms and place all force on the elbows leading through the lats.

Leg Routines
Forced reps+Negatives+Static holds

Machine leg press-1x12/3/2/4
Performance:Use a weight that leads to failure at 12 reps. Have two assistants aid in the completion of 3 forced reps followed by 2 negative reps. Increase the weight slightly and have your assistant lift the weight into position for you at the point of maximum contraction, which is the ¾ mark. Do a total of 4 static holds. It will be necessary to reduce the weight 10% on each successive hold due to muscle fatigue. Note the addition of a second assistant, which is necessary due to the heavy weights in the leg press.

Extended slow reps+Negatives+ Superslow reps

Machine hack squat-1x1/3/4
Performance:Use a weight that allows a max effort for one complete rep using a 30/30 rep cadence. Begin with the positive portion(concentric) before lowering. Increase the weight 30% and do 3 negative reps. Using a rep cadence of 10/4, do a total of 3 super-slow reps to failure. If no hack squat machine is available, a barbell or a pair of dumbbells may be used.

Rest-pause+Negatives+Static holds

Leg press-1x1(6)/4/4
Performance:Use a weight that allows 1 max rep. After a 10-second rest, reduce the weight by one plate and complete an additional rep. Continue for a total of 6 reps. Increase the weight by 30% , have two assistants lift the weight before transferring it to you. Lower to an 8-count. Repeat for a total of 4 negatives. Do a series of 4, 10-second holds with a 10-second rest in-between.

Superslow+Static Holds+Burn reps

Barbell squat-1x4/4/6
Performance: Use a weight that leads to failure at 4 reps using a rep cadence of 10/4. Increase the weight and do 4 max holds for 10-seconds with a 10-second rest in-between. Decrease the weight and do a series of 6 burn reps at the top of the movement. Have spotters and a full squat cage in case of an uncontrollable drop of the weight.

Forced reps+Negatives+Static holds

Machine press-1x6/3/2/4
Performance:Use a weight that leads to failure at 6 reps. Have an assistant aid in the completion of 3 forced reps followed by 2 negative reps. Increase the weight slightly and have your assistant lift the weight into position for you at the point of maximum contraction, which is the pre-lockout position. Do a total of 4 static holds. It will be necessary to reduce the weight 10% on each successive hold due to muscle fatigue.

Extended slow reps+Negatives+ Superslow reps

Cable machine press-1x1/4/4
Performance:Use a weight that allows a max effort for one complete rep using a 30/30 rep cadence. Begin with the positive portion(concentric) before lowering. Increase the weight 30% and do 4 negative reps. Using a rep cadence of 10/4, do a total of 3 super-slow reps to failure.

Rest-pause+Negatives+Static holds

Machine press-1x1(6)/4/4
Performance:Use a weight that allows 1 max rep. After a 10-second rest, reduce the weight by one plate and complete an additional rep. Continue for a total of 6 reps. Increase the weight by 30% , have two assistants lift the weight before transferring it to you. Lower to an 8-count. Repeat for a total of 4 negatives. Do a series of 4, 10-second holds with a 10-second rest in-between.

Superslow+Static Holds+Burn reps

Cable machine upright row-1x5/3/6
Performance: Use a weight that leads to failure at 5 reps using a rep cadence of 10/4. Increase the weight and do 3 max holds for 10-seconds with a 10-second rest in-between. Decrease the weight and do a series of 6 burn reps at the top of the movement.

Triceps Routines

Forced reps+Negatives+Static holds

Machine triceps dips-1x6/3/2/4
Performance:Use a weight that leads to failure at 6 reps. Have an assistant aid in the completion of 3 forced reps followed by 2 negative reps. Increase the weight slightly

and have your assistant press the machine arms into position for you at the point of maximum contraction, which is the pre-lockout position. Do a total of 4 static holds. It will be necessary to reduce the weight 10% on each successive hold due to muscle fatigue.

Extended slow reps+Negatives+ Superslow reps

Cable machine press-downs-1x1/4/4
Performance:Use a weight that allows a max effort for one complete rep using a 30/30 rep cadence. Begin with the positive portion(concentric) before raising the rope handle. Increase the weight 30% and do 4 negative reps. Using a rep cadence of 10/4, do a total of 3 super-slow reps to failure.

Rest-pause+Negatives+Static holds

Machine overhead triceps extension-1x1(6)/4/4
Performance:Use a weight that allows 1 max rep. After a 10-second rest, reduce the weight by one plate and complete an additional rep. Continue for a total of 6 reps. Increase the weight by 30% , have two assistants lift the weight before transferring it to you. Lower to an 8-count. Repeat for a total of 4 negatives. Do a series of 4, 10-second holds with a 10-second rest in-between.

Superslow+Static Holds+Burn reps

Cable triceps kickbacks-1x5/3/6
Performance: Use a weight that leads to failure at 5 reps using a rep cadence of 10/4. Increase the weight and do 3 max holds for 10-seconds with a 10-second rest in-between. Decrease the weight and do a series of 6 burn reps at the top of the movement.

Biceps Routines

Forced reps+Negatives+Static holds

Barbell curls-1x6/3/2/4
Performance:Use a weight that leads to failure at 6 reps. Have an assistant aid in the completion of 3 forced reps followed by 2 negative reps. Increase the weight slightly and have your assistant press the machine arms into position for you at the point of maximum contraction, which is the pre-lockout position. Do a total of 4 static holds. It will be necessary to reduce the weight 10% on each successive hold due to muscle fatigue.

Cable machine palms-facing pull-downs-1x1/4/4
Performance:Use a weight that allows a max effort for one complete rep using a 30/30 rep cadence. Begin with the positive portion(concentric) before letting the weight lower back to the stack. Increase the weight 30% and do 4 negative reps. Using a rep cadence of 10/4, do a total of 3 super-slow reps to failure.

Rest-pause+Negatives+Static holds

Seated inclined dumbbell curls-1x1(6)/4/4
Performance:Use a weight that allows 1 max rep. After a 10-second rest, change to dumbbells that are 5 lbs lighter and complete an additional rep. Continue for a total of 6 reps while reducing the dumbbells by 5 lbs each time. Increase the weight by 30% , have two assistants lift the weight before transferring it to you. Lower to an 8-count. Repeat for a total of 4 negatives. Do a series of 4, 10-second holds with a 10-second rest in-between using dumbbells heavy enough for maximum effort.

Superslow+Static Holds+Burn reps

Cable overhead curls-1x5/3/6
Performance: This exercise is done by setting the cable handle high overhead and curling downward to your chin either with a single handle or rope handle. Use a weight that leads to failure at 5 reps using a rep cadence of 10/4. Increase the weight and do 3 max holds for 10-seconds with a 10-second rest in-between. Decrease the weight and do a series of 6 burn reps at the top of the movement.

Abdominals

Superslow+Static Holds+Burn reps

Machine crunches-1x10/3/6
Performance: Use a weight that leads to failure at 10 reps using a rep cadence of 10/4. Increase the weight and do 3 max holds in the peak contraction portion for 10-seconds with a 10-second rest in-between. Decrease the weight and do a series of 6 burn reps at the max contraction part of the movement.

Rolling Static Partials+Static Holds

Machine crunches-1x10/4
Performance: Use a weight that leads to failure at 10 reps using a rep cadence of 2/8. Crunch down normally then during the negative do a short burst of burn reps followed by a static hold, lower the machine arm further then do another series of burn reps

followed by a static hold. Continue in this fashion until 10 reps to failure have been completed. Do four static holds, holding the weight for 10 seconds each time.

Calves

Superslow+Static Holds+Burn reps

Toe presses on leg press machine-1x12/3/6
Performance: Use a weight that leads to failure at 12 reps using a rep cadence of 10/4. Increase the weight and do 3 max holds in the peak contraction portion for 10-seconds with a 10-second rest in-between. Decrease the weight and do a series of 6 burn reps at the max contraction part of the movement.

Extended slow reps+Negatives+ Superslow reps

Standing calf raises-1x1/4/4
Performance:Use a weight that allows a max effort for one complete rep using a 30/30 rep cadence. Begin with the positive portion(concentric) before letting the weight lower back to the stack. Increase the weight 30% and do 4 negative reps. This will entail having one or two partners raising the machine arm for you allowing you to use max weight for the lowering phase. Using a rep cadence of 10/4, do a total of 3 super-slow reps to failure.

These are great examples of extremely intense routines using only one set per muscle group trained. These require all out effort to maximize your muscle gains and make big inroads to your recuperate ability, both your overall system and each individual muscle. Therefore only use these routines sparingly or you will quickly over-train I recommend using the extreme intensity program for two weeks then switching to failure training for two weeks before reverting back. Each muscle should be trained no more than once every 10 days to give yourself adequate rest. Depending on conditioning, age and natural recuperative ability, you may require more days in-between workouts. It may take a little of trial and error to determine your ideal schedule.

Building A Strong Grip

We all know that it is imperative to have a strong grip when lifting weights, or in daily life, giving one the ability to grip objects safely. But what is the best way to produce gains in strength for this area?

The forearm muscle group is the one responsible for grip strength. There are several functions of the forearm muscles including gripping objects, curling the fist upward and lifting the hand backward in a reverse motion. Therefore, we have to train each of these areas for complete forearm development.

To build gripping and crushing strength, pinch grip a barbell plate on the
outside rim and hold it off the floor for as long as you can. Increase the weight as strength gains permit. To do this safely, hold the plate over a floor that is protected by gym padding and leave an open area in case you happen to drop the weight.

Another great tool is a gripper. Use a quality, professional one like Iron Grips or one of the other brands available in a weight lifting store and avoid the ones being sold in department stores as they don't give sufficient resistance and wear out quickly. Since forearm muscles are used to high reps squeeze the gripper for 20-30 reps per set. Do one set using an overhand grip, one using an underhand grip and one with an extended, or straight grip. A tennis ball is a great tool to use to build crushing strength. Squeeze the ball as hard as you can for 15 seconds then release. Do a total of 15 reps per hand.

To increase your curling strength, use a barbell or dumbbell to do wrist curls, curling the weight up as far as you can. Repeat for 15 reps. Use a reverse wrist curl to build up the outside portion of your forearm. Reverse barbell curls are a nice alternative to reverse wrist curls and train the attachment between the forearm and biceps muscles.

A great exercise to build up overall forearm strength is wrist roller wind-ups. Use a handle with a rope attached. Clip a weight plate to the end of the rope and wind up the rope until it is fully wound. Let the plate back to the floor and repeat. Do three complete wind-ups.

A sample workout for complete forearm and grip development is:

Reverse Wrist Curls- 1x 12 reps
Gripper squeezes-1x 25 each underhand, overhand, straight grip
Wind-Ups- 1x complete cycle

DOMS- Delayed Muscle Soreness

What causes DOMS, delayed onset muscle soreness? Why does it usually get worse the second day after you train?

It was once thought that DOMS was caused by the buildup of lactic acid after a hard exercise session or when the trainee was unaccustomed to training and "overdid" it. Newer research has led researchers to believe that it is caused by micro tears in the muscle(s) that were trained during the workout a day or two before the soreness occurred.

Training while sore can increase the soreness and pain felt, although training with moderate intensity helps to flush blood and nutrients into the muscle, minimizing

soreness in many cases. This is due to the muscle being able to rebuild itself
faster with the incoming protein, vitamins and minerals. Remember to drink plenty of water to flush out waste products that result from your training and to replenish fluid lost. Muscle is comprised of 75% water so it is very important to maintain a proper water balance.

Micro tears in your muscles after training are beneficial because your body overcompensates for the minor damage to your muscles by rebuilding them stronger than they were previous to your workout. Stronger muscles are the result, so don't be overly concerned with the soreness felt. As you become more conditioned the soreness will become a thing of the past or at least won't be as acute as it was when you first began training.

If you change your training routine, adding new exercises or changing the reps, sets or intensity, you will often become slightly sore the next day and more so the following day. This is because you experience inflammation which increases the second day as your body adjusts to the micro tears.

One way to minimize the pain and inflammation is to take an over the counter pain medication like Motrin or Advil. These two are great for reducing inflammation and pain. Another great option is the herb Turmeric, which contains the active ingredient Curcumin. Medical studies have shown Turmeric to be as effective at reducing inflammation as the prescription medication Celebrex.

Celebrex was taken from the market by the FDA after it was shown to be a cause of heart attacks and cardiovascular disease. It has returned to the market despite these dangers, so I would opt for a safer natural medicine. By reducing muscle inflammation, you speed up healing which causes your body to increase muscle faster, allowing you to resume training more quickly.

Give your muscles adequate rest between training sessions so your body can rebuild muscle tissue, restore and build on strength levels so you will be able to train with heavier weights the next time. If you find yourself training with less weight than the previous session, you have trained before your muscles have fully recovered and need to increase the days between workouts.

Shocking Methods To Accelerate Muscle Gains

When you first begin training gains come easily. It seems like everything you do leads to increased muscle strength and size. After you have been training for awhile your workouts tend to become stale as you continue to do the same exercises,sets and reps week in and week out. The problem is you have become too predictable in your

workouts leading to stalled muscle gains.
Your body is very efficient at maintaining the status quo-it will try anything it can to keep the amount of muscle on your body the same. This is because of the high energy cost to increase muscle mass and sustain it. This makes it necessary to change things up from time to time to reignite muscle gains.

Maybe you have searched through the various muscle magazines in search of the perfect training routines to begin experiencing new muscle gains. The question is what is the best way to freshen up your workouts, breathe new life into them and start growing new muscle again?

Changing The Time Under Tension

Try changing the rep count or time under tension to see what effect that has. If you have been consistently doing 6-8 reps per set, try some sets with 8-10 reps or even 12-15. Keep in mind the ideal time under tension depends on the muscle fiber type of the muscle. If the muscle is predominately fast twitch, tut should be in the 40-60 second range; if it is mostly slow twitch, keep your tut at 60-90 seconds. Altering the tut will spark new growth because the body becomes used to the current training being done and works hard at keeping everything the same unless you force it out of homeostasis by giving it new stimulus.

New Exercises

Delete exercises you have been using for awhile and replace them with ones you haven't done recently. Learn new exercises from trainers, fellow trainees or bodybuilding books or magazines.

Combo Rows-This exercise is a combination of the bent over lateral raise and upright row exercises. Stand and lean slightly forward. Hold a dumbbell in each hand, palms facing in front of each thigh. Row the weights up while keeping your forearms aimed vertically. Stop at chest level;your elbows should be angled toward the ceiling. Pause for a second then return to the beginning position.

As with any new exercise, begin with a lighter weight and avoid training hard until you have mastered the form of the exercise. A good way to integrate this exercise into your shoulder routine is to combine it with a pressing movement like dumbbell presses as a pre-exhaust super-set. To do this, begin with a set to failure of combo rows followed by a set of shoulder presses to failure. Do this super-set with no rest between exercises. If you rest as little as five seconds between sets, your muscles' regain 50% of their strength, which defeats the purpose of the pre-exhaust variable.

Bicep Blaster Curls-Made popular in the movie Pumping Iron, these use a specially 58 -designed metal brace which is placed in front of the body to immobilize the upper arm to force perfect form in the bicep curl. I have found these to be helpful when training beginning bodybuilders but they are useful to even the most experienced athlete. After placing the strap around your neck and the brace against your abdomen, grab a weight and curl it while keeping your upper arm against the brace. You will feel how this tool changes the curl after doing an intense set of these.

Cable Cross Triceps Press-downs-Stand in front of a cable crossover machine. Attach single rope handles to each side. Cross the cables in an 'x' and press them down and out at an angle until fully extended. Pause for one second while flexing your triceps hard before returning to the start position. Repeat.

This exercise is a great modification of the standard triceps press-down exercise and hits the muscle from a different angle, which gives a great muscle growth stimulus.

Reverse Leg Lunges-Hold a dumbbell in your left hand while standing shoulder-width apart. Take a deep step back with your left leg while squatting down. Step back to the beginning position and change the weight to your right hand. Do the same deep step back with your right leg and squat down. Continue until you have completed the desired reps.

This exercise is a nice variation of the standard leg lunge and works the legs from a different direction.

In addition to adding or replacing exercises in your training routine, there are many other ways to change your program and initiate new growth in your muscles.

Using Different Hand Placements

By changing the positioning of your hands on the bar, handle or attachment, you hit a muscle from different angles while performing an exercise. This activates fibers not used during previous applications of the exercise. For example, if you use a narrow grip during lat pull-downs, you stimulate your lat muscles one way; another way if you use a mid-grip and yet another way if a wide grip is used.

The same goes for barbell curls-while the curl works the entire bicep muscle- using different grip placement changes the way the weight affects the muscle. This adds variety to your training and literally forces the muscle to grow because of the new demands placed on it.

Try curling with a four inch hand spacing. Place your hands two inches from center and do a set of curls. Now move your hands two more inches apart and complete another set of curls. Do a set of curls using a standard grip spacing. Lastly, place your hands wide on the bar and complete a set of curls. Feels a lot different doesn't it?

Apply the same strategy to machine or barbell rows for the back and bench presses for the chest. The opportunities to change your exercises are nearly endless.

Training Legs Before Smaller Muscle Groups

Scientific research has shown that muscle growth response to exercise increases when the leg muscles are trained prior to other muscles. This is because a much greater release of testosterone and human growth hormone occur when leg training is done as opposed to training smaller muscle groups such as arms and abs. Since legs constitute a much larger muscle mass, they stimulate a larger amount of test and hgh.

To put this into practice, do a set of leg extensions followed by a set of leg presses and a set of hack squats-all sets to failure. Now do your typical arm routine, training all sets to failure.

Be sure to track your progress as you strive to constantly increase the weight you're able to use. Aim to add 1-5 pounds to the bar or machine every workout. That way you avoid adding too much weight at one time, which could lead to failure to complete an exercise.

Try micro-loading by adding special, 1-1.5 pound plates to the bar or machine. This is effective because it makes the bar feel as if no new weight has been added. Over a year you will be able to add substantial weight. I used arms in this example but any other muscle group can be trained after legs with the same results.

Another strategy to re-invigorate new growth in muscles is shocking. There are a number of ways to shock your muscles including high reps/sets, the use of new exercises and the use of HIT variables not used in normal training. The reason for using shocking methods is the body's impressive ability to acclimate itself to training methods used by bodybuilders, no matter how intense they are. Thus, it becomes necessary to change things pretty regularly to avoid becoming stale in your training.

Doing the same exercises in the same manner day in and day out reduces the potential for new muscle growth because it increases muscle complacency due to lack of new stimulation.

Experienced bodybuilders know this fact and have made good use of stutter reps, negative-only, the 21-method, one-and-a-quarter reps, target ROM training, etc. – changing up workouts to continuously forcing their muscles to adapt to the new workload being placed on them. The same is true of altering rep cadence or speed.

Successful bodybuilders will routinely alter specific exercise demands to cycle methods to keep the muscles guessing -and growing. One method for doing that is changing from moderately fast movements to very slow ones as this can have a significant change in muscle response, and will keep the body guessing and on edge, to encourage a higher level of training response.

I am going to outline both high volume and HIT as they both are effective at stimulating the muscles by temporary overreaching. We will be over-training but only for a short period of time. If shocking were used for too long a time it would lead to the effects of over-training, which were discussed previously.

High Volume Shocking Method

The first type of shocking method I will outline is the high volume approach. There will be excessive sets and reps while on this program, which will inflict the body with resource-draining stress levels. DO NOT do more training than is recommended.

Chest

- Dumbbell bench press-8x15-25 (Vary the rep count in the sets so some are 15,some are 18 and 25. Rest one minute between sets.)
- Standing bar dips-8x10-15 (Rest one minute between sets.)
- Cable cross-over-8x25-30 (Rest one minute between sets.)

Back

- Nautilus pullovers-8x20-25 (Rest one minute between sets. Vary rep count.)
- Barbell rows-8x15-20 (Rest one minute between sets. Vary rep count.)
- Cable pull-downs-8x20-25 (Rest one minute between sets. Vary rep count.)
- Back hyper-extensions-8x25 (Rest one minute between sets.)

Legs

- Barbell squats-8x25-30 (Rest one minute between sets. Vary rep count.)
- Dumbbell leg lunges-8x25 each leg (Rest one minute between sets.)
- Leg curls-10x30 (Rest one minute between sets.)

Shoulders

- Machine lateral raises-8x20-25 (Rest one minute between sets.)
- Shoulder rotations with dumbbell-8x20-25 each direction (Rest one minute between sets)
- Machine presses-8x20-25 (Rest one minute between sets.)

Triceps

- Angled triceps extension-8x25-30 (Rest one minute between sets.)
- Seated overhead triceps extensions-8x20-25 (Rest one minute between sets.)
- Close-grip machine bench presses-8x25-30 (Rest one minute between sets.)

Biceps

- Concentration curls-8x25-30 (Rest one minute between sets)
- Barbell curls-8x25-30 (Rest one minute between sets)
- Palms-forward barbell rows-8x30

Please note: On the larger muscles, I have used a total of four exercises; smaller muscles have three.

Please forgive me for the excessive repeating of "Rest one minute between sets." I want to make sure everything is done correctly including rest periods,etc. It isn't necessary to end all sets at failure but push hard and exert as close to 100% effort as possible. What we're looking to achieve here is
excessive work-done on a short term basis-no longer than two weeks to "shock" the muscles into new growth.

Even though I outlined routines for every muscle group, only use shocking methods on one muscle at a time. All other training muscles should be trained normally while the muscle being shocked is trained with one of these routines for two weeks.

Giant Set Routine

Giant sets are a great way to condense a lot of work into a short period of time. Four or more sets of different exercises for the same muscle group are done in succession, with no rest in-between. Take all sets to failure. I like combining weight machines with free weights and sometimes alternate between machines and free weights or between compound and isolation exercises.

- Barbell curls-1x10
- Incline dumbbell curls-1x12

- Seated behind-neck cable curls-1x15
- Palms-facing pull-downs-1x8
- Negative-only chin-ups-1x8 (Step up to the high position using your legs only. Lower yourself to a count of 8.)

Do one complete giant set. If all sets are stopped at failure, you will be over -training. This must be done on an irregular basis, i.e. once or twice per month or you will be compromising your gains. Use this routine as a higher-set shocking routine.

HIT Shocking Method

The other shocking method available is the HIT, high intensity method. Like other HIT training, it is based on the use of maximum effort, low volume sets. While set count will be increased slightly, the main difference is the addition of numerous HIT variables to increase the intensity level to the point of overreaching. If this level of intensity were maintained, it would result in gross over-training and loss of muscle.

As explained in the section on high volume shocking, focus on one muscle group at a time, for no longer than two weeks. Use standard training routines for all other muscles and resume normal training for the muscle being focused on during the shocking period. All sets need to be done with maximum effort to be effective.

Chest

- Machine bench press-1x6+4 forced reps+ 4 negative reps+ 3 static holds

End the set at failure with six reps, complete four forced reps and four negative reps with the assistance of a partner, reduce the weight 20% and do three static holds, with a 10-second rest in-between.

- Standing bar dips-1x8 negative-only+3 static holds

Add a dip belt with extra weight and do a set of eight negative only reps. Reduce the weight and do three static holds, 10-seconds each, one at the top,mid-point and bottom.

- Pek dek flyes-1x8+4 forced reps+ 4 static holds

Complete eight reps; do four forced reps, and after reducing the weight, do a series of four static holds.

Legs

- Barbell squats-1x12+4 static holds

After completing twelve reps, reduce the weight 20% and do a series of four static holds.

- Leg press-1x10+6 forced reps+4 static holds.

Use your arms to give yourself forced reps. Reduce the weight 20% and do four static holds.

- Leg extensions-1x12+8 negative reps at end of set.

Reduce the weight 25% and have a partner lift the machine's arms to the extended position and transfer the weight to you. Lower to a count of 8.

Back

- Dead-lifts-1x8
- Machine rows-1x8+4 forced reps+6 negative-only reps

Have a partner assist you in completion of four forced reps. Your partner should lift the weight and transfer it to you for the negatives.

- Medium grip pull-downs-1x8+4 forced reps+4 negative reps

Shoulders

- Bent-over delt raises-2x12+4 forced reps
- Standing side lateral raises-2x12+4 negative reps+4 static holds
- Machine Presses-2x10+4 forced reps+4 static holds

Triceps

- Seated machine dips-2x12+ 8 negative reps
- Dumbbell triceps kickbacks-2x12+4 forced reps+3 static holds

Biceps

- Machine preacher curls-2x10+4 forced reps+ 3 static holds
- Barbell curls-2x12 negative only

There shouldn't be any rest between sets as soon as conditioning makes it possible. This keeps the intensity at a premium. Do the first exercise, the second,third, if applicable, and repeat until the required training schedule is done. As with the higher volume method, use the shocking method with one muscle group at a time to avoid exhaustion.

Continue for two weeks before reverting to a normal training routine. Often its best to have a complete layoff from any training for 7-10 days after shocking muscles to allow the entire body's energy systems to fully recuperate.

Isolation and Compound Exercise List

The following is a list of isolation (single joint) and compound (multi-joint) exercises for each muscle group:

Legs-compound- squat, leg press, dumbbell squat, sissy squat, hack squat, lunge
Isolation- leg extension, leg curl, calf raise, seated calf raise, donkey calf raise, toe presses on leg press machine

Back-compound- barbell/dumbbell rows, end barbell rows, machine rows, pull-downs, dead-lift, stiff-legged dead-lifts, good mornings, kettlebell swings, pull-up, chin-up
Isolation- Stiff-arm pull-down, dumbbell pullovers, machine pullovers, ab strap bent arm pull-downs, seated reverse machine flyes, Nautilus behind neck machine, side cable lat pull-downs

Chest- compound- bench press, incline bench press, decline bench press, dumbbell bench press, incline dumbbell bench press, decline dumbbell bench press, push-ups
Isolation- dumbbell flyes, incline dumbbell flyes, decline dumbbell flyes, low pulley cable crossovers, mid pulley cable crossovers, high pulley cable crossovers, band low flyes, band mid flyes, band high flyes, pek dek, machine flyes

Shoulders- compound- barbell presses, dumbbell presses, band presses, snatch, clean and jerk
Isolation- Front deltoid raise, side deltoid raise, bent-over deltoid raise, front cable raise, side cable raise, bent-over cable raise, dumbbell rotations, upright rows, seated machine lateral raise, Arnold press, band pull-apart, cable internal rotation, face pull

Biceps- compound- cable pull-downs, bent-over forward grip rows, palms-up cable row
Isolation- barbell curl, dumbbell curl, cable curl, band curl, preacher curl, concentration curl, incline dumbbell curl, bench dumbbell curl, single-arm rope curl behind neck, two-arm rope curls behind neck, rope curl, lying bar curl, lying rope curl, hammer curl, machine curl, barbell reverse curl, reverse machine curl, zottman curl, cross-body hammer curl, drag curl

Triceps- compound- close-grip bench press, bar dips, bench dips, machine dips, narrow push-ups
Isolation- cable press-down, reverse-grip cable press-down, cable push-down, rope press-down, seated dumbbell triceps extension, lying triceps extension, machine triceps extension, standing 30-degree cable triceps extension, dumbbell triceps kickback

Forearms- isolation- barbell wrist curl, dumbbell wrist curl, barbell reverse wrist curl, rope wind-ups, grip squeeze, reverse grip squeeze, ball squeeze, side forearm rotation, side reverse forearm rotation, plate pinch grip, barbell finger curl, one-sided dumbbell wrist rotations

Abdominals- isolation- sit-ups, ab crunches, ab machine crunches, ab wheel roll, lying leg raises, hanging leg raises, machine leg raises, inversion bench sit-ups, side rotations, side machine rotations

Bonus Section

Using Strength Bands To Build Power And Size

There are many effective tools when it comes to the development of muscle size and strength. The tried and true ones like barbells,dumbbells and machines have proven themselves effective for many,many years.

A tool that has been around for a number of years,and is increasing in popularity, is strength bands. Power-lifters have used them to build explosive power in their lifts by attaching them to the bar using special collars on one end and a hook on a power rack on the other end. They help eliminate weak links,or sticking points,in your lifts by increasing tension at the zone where these occur.

Let's take a look at their use in the bench press. As a bar advances,a sticking point is reached at the position where the triceps take over most of the effort,the 50% mark. To work through this a power-lifter places a band on the bar and a hook at the bottom of the rack and does a set with heavy weight and low reps, usually 3-5. The resistance increases as the band stretches, forcing the lifter to squeeze every ounce of effort toward completing the rep. This method is used to build explosive strength for power-lifting competitions. This can also be used to help a bodybuilder increase the tension on a muscle while training.

Reverse band training is used to decrease resistance as the bar advances to the sticking point in a lift. Using the bench press as an example again, one end of a band would be attached to the barbell and the other to a hook at the top of the power rack. As the bar reaches the central sticking point, the band aids the lifter through by helping to lift the bar. Since there are many different resistance levels in bands, the assistance can be tailored to the strength level of the athlete and can be reduced as strength levels increase.

Bands are great to use without barbells too. Try a set of concentration curls with a band and you'll feel an increase in tension as the band stretches,maximizing at the point of full contraction. This causes the recruiting of a large number of muscle fibers,which leads to more muscle damage and better results. Since there are no bad leverage points due to constant tension from the bands,which becomes greater as the band is stretched,almost any exercise can be made more effective with their use.

I like to "mix in" band work with machines and free weights to take advantage
of each tool's training advantages. An example is barbell curls supersetted with lying overhead band curls. Attach one end of the band to the top of a pulley machine and lie on a flat bench placed under the band. Curl the band down with both hands until your hands reach your forehead. Squeeze your biceps hard for one second before returning to the top. The resistance in this exercise increases dramatically as it progresses and builds to a peak at the end. Other exercises that build to peak contraction are band chest crossovers,band concentration curls,band rows and band triceps press-downs.

Exercises To Do To Build Power And Size With Bands

There are many exercise movements that bodybuilders do with traditional free weight equipment that can be duplicated with bands. Let's take a look at some exercises you can do to increase overall power and size.

Band squats-Start- Start-Grasp two large bands while standing on the the end. Place the other ends over your shoulders. Action- Lower yourself to below parallel,pause one second then push up against the resistance until fully upright.

Band rows-These are similar to barbell rows. Start-Stand on the middle of a band either single or double thickness. Action-Grasp both ends and row to your lower chest,pause one second then return.

Band chest press-Start-Attach one long band or two individual bands to a wall or doorway. Action-Brace yourself before pressing the bands to pre-lockout position,pause one second,return.

Band dead-lift- Start-Hold a band in the same way you did for the band rows. Action- Using a standard grip,dead-lift the band as you would a barbell.

Band press-Start-Attach a band to the floor or stand on the middle of the band. Action- While sitting, press both ends of the band overhead.

Band curls-Start-Attach one end of the band to the floor while holding the other end. Action-Curl the band up to the top,hold for one second before returning.

Band triceps extensions-Start-Sit on a chair while standing on one end of a band. Action-While keeping your elbow fixed along the side of your head,extend the band overhead,pause one second before returning.

Even though these exercises are very similar to comparable barbell exercises,the bands keep constant tension on the muscles, which increases the more the band stretches. This tension emphasizes the negative,or eccentric portion of the rep.   67

Research has shown negative-emphasized training breaks down muscles more than the positive,or concentric does. There is a greater release of growth hormone from negatives as well,leading to more muscle size increases.

Try the following routine as a full body circuit:

Band dead-lift-1x12
Band Squat-1x15
Band bench press-1x12
Band rows-1x10
Band press-1x10
Band curls-1x10
Band triceps extensions-1x12

Complete this circuit once initially,with no rest between exercises. If ending sets before muscular failure,do a second circuit after a 90 second rest. This is great for building both strength and cardio conditioning. To maximize size/strength increases,do the complete circuit once,ending all sets at muscular failure.

Bonus Q &A Section

Q: Is spot reduction of fat possible if I do a lot of high repetition abdominal work such as sit-ups or ab crunches?

A: No. While it has been shown there is a minor amount of fat spot reduction during abdominal exercises, it is such a small amount it would be impossible to notice. A better method of reducing body fat is to eat a healthy diet consisting of lean meats, vegetables, whole grains and an appropriate amount of healthy fats such as fish, olive and canola oils while using a training routine of maximum effort multi-joint exercises such as barbell squats, leg presses, bench presses and dead lifts. These exercises train the large muscle groups of the body. Since it takes a sizable amount of calories to fuel these muscles, you will lose much more fat with these movements than endless amounts of abdominal training.

Q: What are good exercises for women to get rid of flabby arms?

A: A common problem area for women is flabby arms, especially at the back of the arm. The muscle at the back of the arm, the triceps muscle, becomes weak and flabby as a result of being untrained. Some great exercises are triceps kickbacks using a dumbbell, bar dips and close-grip bench presses. Triceps kickbacks are done by grabbing a pair of

dumbbells, and while bending forward, extending the dumbbells back   68
while keeping your elbows pinned to your sides. To perform bar dips using parallel bars, lower yourself down to get a full stretch before pressing yourself to the top. Maintain an erect position during this movement for best result. Close-grip bench presses are done while lying on a flat bench. Press two dumbbells straight up from your chest until your arms are nearly fully extended. Do a total of 10-12 repetitions of each exercise.

Q: Does using a wobbly board or stability ball during training exercises increase the effectiveness of my training routine?

A: These pieces of equipment are being promoted by various groups as ways to increase the strength of your "stability muscles." While at first glance they may seem helpful to use during your training, they are actually very dangerous. There are instances where trainees have been using Bosu balls while bench pressing and have rolled off the ball and injured themselves badly.

Your so-called stabilizer muscles are actually your abdominal, lower back and other nearby muscles. They are best trained not with an unpredictable ball but more traditional exercises such as sit-ups, ab crunches, side bends and machine or free weight rotational exercises. Don't do endless sets of high repetitions but instead do a more moderate routine such as one set of 15 repetitions of each of the above exercises.
Q: Which exercises are the best for developing and toning the muscles in my legs?

A: Leg extensions are a great exercise to use as they isolate the thigh muscles in the upper leg area. Sit on a leg extension machine and extend both legs outward to full extension. Pause for a second then return. Squats using a barbell or smith machine are great for working the entire legs if a low enough descent is done. It is best for someone beginning training to use a smith machine due to safety concerns. Lying leg curls are a great exercise to isolate the hamstring muscles on the back of the leg. To develop the lower leg (calf) hold a dumbbell at your side. Lower your foot all the way down while standing on a block with the ball of your foot and extend your foot to the top. Do 15-20 repetitions on these.

Q: How do I use kettlebells in my workout routine?

A: Kettlebells, while a very popular training tool today, have been around for about 350 years. Though similar to dumbbells, they can be used in many unique ways to train every muscle group in the body effectively. Some common movements are kettlebell swings, lunges, squats, clean and press and rows. If you attend a kettlebell training session you will observe instructors and trainees swinging the kettlebells in an effort to use heavier weights. This is both dangerous due to the pressure placed on the tendons and joints because of the momentum and ineffective because the effort is reduced on the muscles.

The ideal way to use kettlebells is with a deliberate, steady motion. This concentrates the resistance on the muscles being worked.

A basic workout is as follows:
Kettlebell swings
Clean and press
One-handed rows
Clean and squat
Figure 8's
Triceps extensions
Curls

This regimen uses all of the body's major muscle groups in a functional way, which mimics the natural movements of the body. This coordinates the body's muscles with each other, leading to better health in daily life and increased performance in sports.

Begin by using both hands with one kettlebell for all of the exercises, and after training for a month or so, begin to alternate between sessions using two hands and one-handed exercises. By using one-handed movements, you will be able to concentrate more on each arm or side of the body, which is beneficial.

Q: Is it possible to get in shape using traditional calisthenics-type exercises?

A: Yes it is. In fact, they are a great addition to free weight, weight machine and kettlebell training routines. One of the most effective methods for obtaining results in your workout program is to change your program around frequently to constantly challenge your muscles and body systems. The human body adapts very quickly to demands imposed on it and will stop responding as soon as this adaptation occurs. Body-weight exercises are a great way to "change up" your routine.

If we go back to our gym class days, we quickly remember push-ups, sit-ups, knee bends, pull-ups, jumping jacks and more.

A good workout routine using these along with free weights is:
- Push ups-use the newer push up bars available at sporting goods stores, 10-15 reps
- Knee bends, 12-15 reps
- Pull-ups, 8-12 reps
- Dumbbell overhead presses, 8 reps
- Dumbbell curls, 10 reps

- Dumbbell triceps overhead extensions, 10 reps
- Dumbbell wrist curls, 15 reps
- Sit-ups or ab crunches, 20 reps

This routine will train your entire body using a combination of compound movements, which use more than one muscle group at a time, and isolation exercises, which train one muscle at a time.

Q: Is weight training a good method of exercise for elderly people?

A: Weight training is an excellent method to help condition a person who is elderly in age. As long as a doctor verifies the individual is in sufficient condition to safely workout and safe training practices are followed, this is an excellent way to tone and strengthen the entire body.

Other forms of exercise such as walking are excellent ways to strengthen the cardiovascular system, but while exercising the muscles of the body, do not exert the same type of force upon the muscles and other tissues of the body as weight training. It has been shown in medical studies that having weight resistance placed upon the bones causes a thickening of the bone structure and an increase in bone density, helping stave off the effects of osteoporosis.

As we age one of the first muscle groups to lose strength are the legs. This is obvious when you observe many of the elderly walking hunched over and having trouble walking. Walkers are used to brace themselves and prevent falls due to weak leg muscles. Much of this could be avoided had the individual trained with weights.

Some great exercises to use to strengthen the legs are squats done with as low a descent as is safe and comfortable, leg presses on a machine, dumbbell lunges, leg extensions and leg curls.

Q: How does brisk walking compare to jogging?

A: There has been research that suggests that taking a brisk walk can be as beneficial as jogging or running if the energy expenditure is comparable. The pulse and breathing rates are certainly higher during running and it takes much less time to cover the same distance but the body is subjected to exercise for a longer time during walking exercise. Numerous injuries can occur during jogging or running because of the hard impact on the joints and other parts of the body. Walking, on the other hand, places very little strain on the body because it is low impact. One way to avoid the impact jogging places on the body is to run on soft surfaces such as grassy trails or sandy beaches.

Q: What is the recommended exercise dosage per day for the average person?

A: It is recommended that every person spend an hour per day engaging in moderate exercise. Tennis, brisk walking, jogging and weight training are excellent examples of beneficial types of exercise to take part in on a daily basis. I recommend avoiding the same exercise every day, as playing tennis daily, would lead to overuse injuries such as tennis elbow. Plus, it makes exercise much more enjoyable if you inject variety in your program.

Q: I'm tight on time. How do I get a good workout in to both tone and strengthen my muscles?

A: If you are unable to spend the proper amount of time training to obtain the best results from your workouts, it is still possible to get some great benefits from a relatively short exercise session. Remember, it is very important to exercise on a regular basis so even if you are not getting the ideal workout time in at least you are getting some exercise.

 Since you aren't going to be able to concentrate on each body part individually, I recommend a routine built on compound exercises such as barbell or dumbbell squats, dead lifts, bench presses and such. Compound exercises train more than one muscle group at a time saving you time over what you would spend doing single muscle exercises.

Compound exercises form the basis of strength gains because they tax the central nervous system more than other exercises, and there is research that suggests they stimulate natural human growth hormone release in the body which can lead to increased muscle strength and development.

The following is a great program to condition the entire body:
- Barbell or dumbbell squats- 1 set of 15 repetitions
- Barbell or dumbbell bench presses- 1 set 12 repetitions
- Barbell or dumbbell rows- 1 set 12 repetitions
- Dumbbell presses- 1 set 12 repetitions
- Lying abdominal crunches- 1 set 15 repetitions

The entire body will be trained with this abbreviated routine and you will quickly realize good results with this program. Warm-up adequately before beginning the work sets to avoid injury. It is important to practice the exercises to get proper form so the effort is focused on the muscles being trained.

Q: What is a good way to build better grip strength? 72

A: To increase your grip strength you need to train your forearm muscles in several different ways. You will need to use a wrist roller, which is a bar with a rope through it that you attach a weight plate to and wind up. Another essential tool is a gripper which comes in different resistance levels. Use a good quality one that will last you.

To build up your holding strength, use a thick bar for some of your lifting. By using a thicker grip you will tax your forearm muscles and increase your holding strength. Lastly, you will need to increase your pinching grip by grabbing a barbell plate using a pinch grip on the edge of the plate. Begin with a light plate and gradually work your way up to heavier weights.

A sample training program using these exercises is as follows:
- Wrist roller- 1 set of 6 windups
- Reverse barbell curls using a thick bar-1 set 15 reps
- Pinch grips- 10-30 second hold

Begin by using a weight in the wrist roller that is challenging to roll up for 6 wind-ups. Hold the bar straight in front of you at arms length. Roll the weight up to the top and release it back down. This constitutes one wind-up.

Attach a thick grip adapter to a standard bar and complete a set of reverse curls, which are done like regular barbell curls with a palms-down grip.
To do a pinch grip simply grab a barbell plate with the ends of your fingers and raise the plate up about two feet while holding it. Gradually increase the size of the plate as your strength increases being careful not to drop the weight on your foot.

Q: What is a good routine to develop my core?

A: Your "core" muscles are comprised of your upper and lower abdominals, side obliques and other muscles in your midsection including your lower back. The best way to train them is with a combination of body-weight exercises, free weights and abdominal and lower back exercise machines.

The core muscles are responsible for the stability of the body while performing both everyday tasks and exercising. An undeveloped midsection will lead to bad posture and injuries. While I advocate using resistance to train these muscles, you must be careful not to use too much resistance to avoid overdeveloping them, which could give one an appearance of having a thick waist.

The weights used should allow you to complete a moderate level of repetitions
per set, somewhere in the range of 12-20. This is ideal for both toning and strengthening
the muscle groups in this region. Begin with a training program consisting of one set of
two exercises for one week. After the first week increase the exercises to three for the
frontal and side abdominals and one for the lower back. Vary the exercises to keep
yourself fresh during your exercise routine.

The following routine will yield good results:
- Lying bent-knee raises 1 set 20 reps
- Ab crunches 1 set 12-20 reps
- Dumbbell side bends 1 set 12 reps per side
- Lower back machine extensions 1 set 12-20 reps

Here is another effective routine:
- Hanging knee raises 1 set 12-20 reps
- Standing opposing toe touches 1 set 15 reps per side
  page 2
- Stiff-legged dead-lifts 1 set 12 reps

Q: How do I use kettlebells to strengthen and tone my leg muscles?

A: Kettlebells are an excellent tool to train not only the leg muscles but also the entire
body. There are several other great tools for training the legs, which we will take a look
at in a future column. As we age our legs lose strength at a more rapid pace than most
other muscles so it is very important to use a regular exercise program that is effective at
building strength in the leg muscles.

It is also important to train the front (thigh) and rear (hamstring) muscles of the legs
evenly to avoid injuries such as hamstring pulls and other common injuries. Before
beginning this or any exercise program for that matter, consult with your doctor to
determine if it is safe for you to exercise.

To train our legs we are going to use a combination of traditional kettlebell exercises and
typical weight training exercises.

A good beginning workout to begin with is as follows:
- Kettlebell swings- 12 repetitions
- Kettlebell clean and squat- 12 repetitions
- Kettlebell leg lunges- 12 repetitions

To do a kettlebell swing, use a stance wider than your shoulders and grab a kettlebell

with both hands. Bend over, and using a smooth movement with no 74
momentum, bring the kettlebell up overhead. Pause for one second then return to the
start position. Repeat.

Kettlebell clean and squats are done by grabbing a kettlebell with both hands, bending
forward and rapidly bringing it to shoulder level in front of you. Squat down to parallel
or below if your knees allow and return. Repeat.

To do a kettlebell lunge, hold the weight in one hand and step forward with the leg on
the same side. Return and repeat with the other leg. Begin by stepping forward with a
normal stride then as you become more advanced increase the length of the stride.

Q: I heard kickboxing training is very good for getting in shape. Can you give me details
on this type of program?

A: Kickboxing training is a very effective method of training and properly done will get
you in top shape fast. This program uses equipment such as heavy bags, speed bags and
other devices that are familiar to anyone who has observed a boxer training on
television, and involves the trainee doing a series of punches and kicks much like karate
usually in three-minute rounds with a minute rest in-between. There are many other
variations but this is the most common.

The heavy bag builds strength and power in your muscles while the various speed bags
increase your reflexes and speed. Substantial calories are burned during this training as it
can be pretty rigorous when performed by an advanced trainee.

A sample training session is:
- Speed bag- 3 minutes

Use a rapid, light, circular punching motion to build speed and co-ordination.
- One minute rest
- Heavy bag- 3 minutes

Alternate punching and kicking blows while increasing your power by striking the
bag in different areas and heights.
- One minute rest
- Floor free –standing reflex bag- 3 minutes

This tool is available at most sporting goods retailers and is an excellent addition to
any home boxing gym. Strike this bag with different style punches using both a speed
and power approach.

- Rope jumping or running in-place- 3 minutes

Repeat this sequence as conditioning permits.

Q: What is the best way to keep my exercise program interesting and avoid boredom?

A: Many people quit an exercising program because they find sticking to a program boring. The best way to avoid this and continue making gains in conditioning is to change your training routine on a regular basis. This not only builds new enthusiasm for training but brings new challenges to your body that it isn't used to experiencing which leads to better results.

Some ways to change your routine include: altering the order of your exercises such as performing bench presses before dumbbell flyes one week and switching the order the next week. Try adding and deleting exercises done for a certain muscle group area. An example is: dumbbell flyes and bench presses for the chest muscles one week and bar dips and incline bench presses the next session.

Another way you can breathe new life into your routine is to workout with a new exercise partner. They may bring new ideas and enthusiasm to your sessions and offer you a friendly challenge during your training.

A great way to quickly learn proper technique and training principles is to hire an experienced personal trainer. Check his or her credentials to ensure that you are getting proper instruction and supervision of your exercise program.

Q: What causes DOMS, delayed onset muscle soreness?

A: It was once thought that DOMS was caused by the buildup of lactic acid after a hard exercise session or when the trainee simply "overdid" it. Newer research has led researchers to believe that it is caused by micro tears in the muscle(s) that were trained during the workout a day or two before the soreness occurred. Training while sore can increase the soreness and pain.

Remember, micro tears in your muscles after training is beneficial because your body overcompensates for the minor damage to your muscles by rebuilding them stronger than they were previous to your workout. Stronger muscles are the result. So don't be overly concerned with the soreness felt. As you become more conditioned the soreness will become a thing of the past.

Q: Are light weights the best way to burn fat?

Many trainers and trainees think that higher reps are necessary to increase the burning of fat during training. Research has shown, however, that it is much more effective to use moderate rep counts to burn fat. Why is this? When you use moderate reps during an exercise you increase the amount of muscle mass.

Muscle tissue burns higher amounts of calories and carbs than other body tissue during exercise and during normal daily activities and raise one's metabolism because of the muscle's energy needs. The body must use more energy (calories) to maintain this muscle mass leading to more fat loss. If one uses lighter weights the muscles don't have to work as hard during training so less energy (calories) are used and less if any muscle is gained.

My recommendation is to perform a circuit of exercises with a concentration on compound exercises. Compound exercises work larger muscle groups at once therefore they burn a higher amount of calories than smaller muscles like the arms, for instance.

Circuit training consists of a series of strength exercises such as leg presses, bench presses, rows and presses. This type of training is great for eliminating boredom in your routine since you will be moving rapidly between exercises. It conditions you by strengthening muscles and improving your aerobic capacity.

A great program is:

- Dead-lifts- 1 set of 15 reps
- Leg presses- 1 set of 12 reps
- Bench presses- 1 set of 12 reps
- Machine pull-downs- 1 set of 12 reps
- Dumbbell presses- 1 set of 10 reps
- Machine crunches- 1 set of 15 reps

Do this circuit with no rest between exercises, rest 2 minutes, then repeat it in the same order. Give this program a try and I think you will agree that it is great for getting you in shape fast!

Q. How do I develop a strong grip?

A. We all know that it is imperative to have a strong grip when lifting weights or in daily life to have the ability to grip objects safely. But what is the best way to produce gains in strength for this area?

The forearm muscle group is the one responsible for grip strength. There are several functions of the forearm muscles including gripping objects, curling the fist upward and lifting the hand backward in a reverse motion. Therefore, we have to train each of these areas for complete forearm development.

To build gripping and crushing strength, pinch grip a barbell plate on the outside rim and hold it off the floor for as long as you can. Increase the weight as strength gains permit. Use a high quality gripper and squeeze it for 20-30 reps. A tennis ball is a great tool to use to build crushing strength. Squeeze the ball as hard as you can for 15 seconds then release. Do a total of 15 reps per hand.

To increase your curling strength, use a barbell or dumbbell to do wrist curls, curling the weight up as far as you can. Repeat for 15 reps. Use a reverse wrist curl to build up the outside portion of your forearm. Another great exercise is a handle with a rope attached. Clip a weight plate to the end of the rope and wind up the rope until it is fully wound. Let the plate back to the floor and repeat. Do about three cycles.

Q: Are there exercises I can do with a medicine ball to get in shape?

A: A medicine ball is a wonderful tool to train your body and improve it. They are available in different weights and textures, designed to improve grip performance.

Originally part of a boxer's training equipment exclusively; it has become very popular among fitness participants. If you've ever watched a show on boxing training you probably have seen a trainer drop a medicine ball on an outstretched boxer's stomach to toughen it up. Medicine ball training for most people has changed dramatically from that.

Not only is it possible to train the entire body with a medicine ball but it is a very effective tool. You can use it to strengthen your leg muscles by holding the medicine ball in front of your chest and doing knee bends, train shoulder muscles by pressing it overhead, and build your arms by curling it. Select a medicine ball weight that allows safe handling of the ball but enough resistance to slow down the speed that you can move it.

A good training program using a fitness ball is:

- Deep knee bends with upward throw
- Side twists
- Forward bends
- Lying press and throw
- Leg lunge with twist
- Overhead press
- Medicine ball push-up
- Overhead triceps press

- Ab crunch

Q: What type of exercise routine is ideal for getting fit?

A: A well rounded routine consisting of aerobic, strength, stretching and balance training should be used regularly to maximize your fitness. Many trainees choose only one or two of these to concentrate on which is a big mistake. You must include all of them to have a well rounded program.

Aerobic exercise, also known as cardio, is the cornerstone of many fitness training programs. Aerobic exercise is any physical activity that uses large muscle groups and increases your heart rate for an extended period of time. Some examples are brisk walking, jogging, running, bike riding and swimming. You should attempt to get in 2.5 hours per week of moderate level aerobic activity per week or slightly over one hour of vigorous aerobic exercise.

Strength training with free weights, machines or bands builds muscle mass and strength and due to its weight bearing effects, builds strong, thicker bones, helping to prevent osteoporosis. The most common tools are free weights such as dumbbells, barbells and kettlebells. They have the advantage of building stability and balance strength over machines. Machines, on the other hand, direct the effort of the training in the proper path for each muscle group to maximize results and tend to be safer to use than free weights. Train 2-3 times per week for best results.

Stretching should be done before each aerobic training session but should be avoided before strength training because recent research has shown that it temporarily weakens the muscles slightly which is not ideal prior to strength training.

Balance is an important part of daily living and is easy to improve through training. Try standing on one foot for extended periods of time, first with one leg in front of you then behind you.

Q. What are the causes of overuse injuries and what can I do to avoid them?

A: Incorrect exercise form and beginning a program doing too much too fast are the most common factors leading to these types of injuries. The best ways to avoid these injuries are to make sure that you are using correct exercise form while training and to do the appropriate volume of exercise during a workout session.

My recommendation is to begin slowly when changing to a new routine until you become acclimated to the new exercises and program. Be open to changing your training program regularly. This is done for numerous reasons, some of which are avoidance of staleness and boredom, and giving new, fresh stimulus to the body.

Add some low impact aerobic exercise such as walking, bicycling, swimming and water aerobics to your strength training to round out your training. Design a new strength training program using compound exercises that train large groups of muscle groups such as squats, bench presses, dead-lifts and barbell presses. Substitute new exercises or old ones that you haven't done in a while for some that you are currently doing to prevent doing the same exercises over and over. This goes a long way to preventing excessive wear and tear on your ligaments and joints which is a major cause of overuse injuries.

Q. I work in an office and am concerned that I sit all day long. I workout at night after I get home. What can I do during the day to get more exercise at my office job?

A: Some medical studies have concluded that it is as important for you to get sufficient exercise during the day as it is for you to train using an organized workout regimen.

This can be difficult if you have a 'desk job' as you mentioned and have to do your work while sitting at a desk. The studies mentioned above found that it is important not to sit continuously for one hour without getting up and moving around. They stated that an individual needs to get up out of their seat every 45 minutes and walk around and be active for several minutes before sitting back in their seat.

This burns calories and increases your metabolism so when you do sit back down you continue to burn calories. It also decreases the fats that build up in your bloodstream, lessening your chance of getting heart disease or some other debilitating disease.

But how do I know if I am exercising enough during the day? One way is to buy an inexpensive pedometer and use it during the day to track the amount of walking that you are doing. Set a realistic daily goal for yourself and keep track of your successes and failures in achieving it. If you don't hit your goal on a given day-don't get discouraged. Pick it up the next day and reward yourself when you obtain your goal-with a healthy food of course!

Q. What are pre-workout drinks and how do they work?

A: There are times when we don't have the energy to put forth the effort needed to succeed in our training. Pre-workout drinks are a supplement that can help with this. These drinks are designed to improve your energy and performance during a workout session, increase strength and endurance, improve focus and nutrient delivery and assimilation. Another effect is a greater flow of blood through the muscles and body. Before trying a pre-workout drink look to see what the ingredients are to make sure they don't conflict with any medications you may be taking and won't cause any problems with any medical conditions you may have. Many of these drinks contain as much caffeine as one cup of coffee so if you aren't able to take caffeine avoid these drinks.

Several amino acids are included and are designed to relax the walls of your blood vessels, causing increased blood flow. This is great for delivery of nutrients to your muscles. Some of the other amino acids aid with protein synthesis into the muscle for increased tissue growth and repair.

Generally powder formulas are best and should be taken 15 minutes prior to your workout for best results. They also come in pill form but aren't absorbed as quickly so they must be taken 30-40 minutes before training. Another advantage to the powder form is it can be stacked with other supplements by adding them to the drink and using a shaker cup to thoroughly mix it prior to drinking.

Q. What does the latest study say about walking and diabetes/sugar control?

A: Walking has always been considered a low-impact, safe exercise for everyone of all ages. Most experts have been recommending regular walking exercise, especially brisk walking. But is there a best time for a walk to maximize its benefits? Recently scientists have found that a brisk 15-minute walk approximately 30 minutes after a meal exerts significant control over the high blood sugar of elderly people.

After a meal blood sugar typically spikes and is driven into the muscle and liver cells by an increase of insulin. As we get older, this system doesn't function as efficiently. Left unchecked, excess blood sugar can contribute to type 2 diabetes and heart disease.

The study examined participant's walking exercise at different times of the day.
They walked on a treadmill for 45 minutes in the morning and afternoon and for 15 minutes within three hours after eating their evening meal. While the morning and afternoon walking was very beneficial, the short, 15-minute walking exercise after the evening meal was more effective at reducing the sugar levels in the bloodstream.

This demonstrates that exercise is great at most any time but maximum benefit can be derived by exercising during a certain time-frame. It was emphasized that the short, 15-minute walking exercise wouldn't be ample to develop much improvement in cardiovascular conditioning though.

Q. Which is better for getting in shape-weight training or aerobics?

A: This is a great question as many people engage in one or the other to improve their health and fitness. You need to perfect your primary fitness goal. Is it to lose weight, build new muscle and strength, improve workout performance or increase endurance? Is it to improve everyday life or to become more competitive at a sport?
After you have identified your primary fitness goal, you need to take a look at the best way to achieve that goal.

If your goal is to lose weight then it is important to include a sufficient amount of cardio to burn more calories and increase your metabolic rate. If your goal is to increase strength and muscle then weight training in any form is the protocol. Remember the more muscle tissue that you carry the more calories that are needed to maintain it. And weight training stimulates the cardiovascular system and increases aerobic capacity just not as much as aerobics.

If you're an athlete and your sport requires intense, short bursts of exertion, like hockey, then a solid HIIT, high intensity interval training program that focuses on 20-30 second bursts of activity (the average hockey shift is 45-60 seconds) would be effective. The ideal program incorporates both aerobic and strength training for best results.

Q. What is Tai Chi and what are the benefits from practicing it?

A: Tai Chi is a form of Chinese martial arts that is renowned for its health benefits. It is very effective at alleviating stress and has been called "meditation in motion", promoting relaxation and inner peace.

The translation of Tai Chi Chuan is "supreme ultimate fist."
There are five distinct styles of Tai Chi, each with their own unique movements. They are Chen, Yang, Wu, Wu-Hao and Sun. Yang is the most popular style and is widely practiced in the U.S.

Not only is Tai Chi safe on the joints but it has been shown to have numerous
health   benefits including increased balance control, fitness and lower blood pressure to name a few. It also improves aerobic capacity, energy and muscle tone. All movements or postures should be practiced with the body completely relaxed, with no tension at all in the muscles.

Proper breath control is taught while doing the postures, leading to a better coordination of body and mind. While it is mostly practiced for the health benefits there is a martial arts side to it so it can be a valuable method of self-defense. So if you are looking for an alternative to karate training, Tai Chi could be what you are looking for.

Q. Can you give me a good workout to improve the muscle tone on the back of my arms?

Many people who have been inactive for some time end up with poor muscle tone on the back of their arm. This is a condition that women are particularly susceptible to. The remedy is a combination of proper diet and the correct exercises. Diet should consist of moderate amounts of complex carbs such as vegetables, fruits and whole grains, lean protein and healthy fats in moderation.

As far as exercise, I recommend cardio, especially bicycling, brisk walking, swimming, tennis and HIIT Training. The best strategy is to alternate the different types of exercise. In other words, play tennis one day, go bicycling the next and swim or walk the following day. Strength training is vitally important, with a concentration on your triceps muscle. This is the muscle in question, the one on the back of your arm that is currently flabby and unconditioned.

I would do a combination of compound exercises and isolation ones. A great program to strengthen and tone up this area is:

- Dumbbell extensions behind head 1x10
- Triceps dumbbell kickbacks 1x 12
- Close-grip bench presses 1x 10

A good band training workout is:

- Band triceps kickbacks 1x 10
- Band triceps press-downs 1x 10
- Band overhead extensions 1x 10

During the first couple of weeks train using one of these workouts once per week.

After that increase your efforts to twice per week, alternating between the
weight and band sessions.

Q. What does a personal trainer do and how can he/she help me with my weight loss and conditioning goals?

Years ago the only people who used, or could afford a personal trainer, were top athletes or movie stars. Today, that isn't the case. Personal training has become the top service offered by gyms. There are one-on-one and group sessions available as well as specialized classes. But what is the best way to choose the right personal trainer and what benefit(s) can he/she provide me in my quest for better conditioning and weight loss or any other goal I may have?

Many people begin a training program on their own, and after a short period of time, become disenchanted with the meager results they achieve. The reason is their lack of experience with diet and training. Because of advancements in exercise physiology, training and exercise have become more specialized, leading to better results in the gym if applied correctly. This is exactly why it is essential to have proper guidance when beginning a training program as well as regular direction to fine tune your workouts for better results.

A good personal trainer will sit down with you to discuss your training and dieting goals and will use this to design a customized training and diet program for you. He/she will give you constructive criticism and encouragement to keep you enthused about your program and will take critical measurements and data to build a journal of achievements, something that should spur you on to more success.

Q. I have flabby calf muscles. What is the best way to tone and strengthen them?

A. The calf muscle is a very dense muscle due to the fact that it is used in everyday walking therefore it is used to high repetition exercise. It thrives on higher rep training with heavy weights to strengthen it.

Your calf muscles provide assistance to your thigh muscles during sporting activities, especially ones where quick turns and fast bursts of speed are needed. In everyday life your calf muscles aid in balance and mobility.

Now, I will outline a program for you to train and develop your calves. Begin by stretching your calves by standing on a block of wood and placing the balls of your feet on the block and letting your heels almost touch the floor. After standing in that position for a couple of minutes begin your strength training by holding a dumbbell in one hand at your side and lowering your heel down toward the floor as before. After getting a

good stretch, lift your heel as high as possible and flex your calf muscle hard.
Repeat for 15-20 reps before changing sides and training your other leg.

Another great exercise, if you have access to a leg press machine, is toe presses. Sit on the seat after selecting a fairly heavy weight and press the footplate out as far as you can with the balls of your feet. Your legs should be locked at the knee to keep the stress on your calves throughout the exercise.

A routine using these two exercises is as follows:
- Calf raises- 1 set of 15-20 reps
- Toe presses- 1 sets of 20 reps
- Stretches-1-2 minutes

Both sets should terminate after reaching muscular failure-where its impossible to complete another full rep.

Do the first set of calf raises and reduce the weight. Rest one minute and do the second set. Do the toe presses in the same way before finishing with a set of stretches.

Q. What is a good overall medicine ball routine to strengthen and tone?

A. Medicine balls are a great tool to strengthen and tone your entire body. They can be used to train your legs, back, chest, shoulders, arms and abdominals. Medicine balls come in different varieties- there are leather balls, vinyl, soft-grip and slam balls. Traditionally they have been used in boxing training but have become very popular with the cross-fit crowd. And for good reason, they are very versatile and effective. They can be thrown to a training partner, tossed up into the air and slammed hard on soft ground or a mat.

A good routine is as follows:

- Medicine ball swing- Stand shoulder width apart; crouch down as you swing the ball down between your legs. Quickly bring the ball up straight overhead.
- Medicine ball squat- Hold the ball at chest height. Squat down low using a shoulder-width stance and press yourself up.
- Medicine ball slam- Lift the ball overhead. Using a swift motion, slam the ball on the ground as hard as you can.
- High throw- Crouch down deep as you hold the ball in front of you. Using an underhand grip throw the ball as high into the air as you can.
- Bent-over row- Lean over until perpendicular to the floor. Row the ball up from the floor to your lower chest
- Overhead triceps extension- Hold the ball behind your head with both hands.

Keeping your elbows at the side of your head press the ball overhead.   85
- Ab crunches- Hold the ball behind your head while in a crunch position on the floor. Do as many crunches as you can.

Q. I've been reading that every minute of daily activity adds up to the 150 minutes per week of US Gov't recommended activity. But that contradicts with what I previously read that it is necessary to exercise vigorously for at least 10 minutes at a time for it to count toward the total. What is correct?

A. A recent study from the University of Utah found that benefits are derived from every minute of moderate -vigorous movement during the day. In fact, for every minute of vigorous movement for men there was a loss of .27 pound and women almost .5 pound. While this may be an insignificant amount on its own, remember it all adds up quickly. The activity has to be vigorous in nature, which means brisk walking for example, as opposed to leisurely strolling along.

Many people think they don't have time for exercising at a gym because they can't spare an hour or two during the week and use that as an excuse for not exercising and bettering their health. With this new finding there is no excuse for not exercising throughout the day. Park farther away from the mall and walk, use the stairs, wash the car by hand-you get the idea!

Q. I have been following a low fat diet for awhile now in an effort to lose weight and be healthier. Now, I'm being told that it is better to eat a higher fat diet that is comprised of healthy fats. What does the latest research show?

A. A recent study conducted in Spain and published online in the New England Journal of Medicine found that a daily dose of healthy fats might be a better choice than a low fat diet. The Mediterranean diet is rich in olive oil, vegetables, fruits, beans, nuts, fish, and a lower consumption of meat and saturated fats. This diet is relatively high in healthy fats, and has proven to have significant health benefits.

The study had participants that were all at an elevated risk for heart disease. Everyone was placed in one of three groups. The first group ate a low fat diet, the second a typical Mediterranean diet while the third ate a Mediterranean diet with extra nuts, such as almonds, hazelnuts and cashews. The research concluded that both groups eating the Mediterranean diet had a 30% reduced risk for heart disease as opposed to the low fat group. So add olives, nuts and other healthy fats to your diet while lowering your consumption of red meats to decrease your risk of contracting heart disease.

Q. Is it beneficial to exercise during my pregnancy?

A. Moderate exercise is very beneficial for both the unborn child and
mother during pregnancy as long as there are no medical restrictions and care is taken to ensure safety for both. A recent study determined that moderate exercise done three times per week for as little as 20 minutes boosted brain development in the newborn baby, something that likely will impact them for their entire lifetime. In fact, inactivity is considered a negative factor during pregnancy because it increases the risk of complications. Being active has shown to reduce obesity rates in children and make the pregnancy more comfortable for the mother.

Water aerobics have been effective at reducing the amount of pain-killing medicines during labor as evidenced in a study at the University of Campinas in Brazil. Only 27% of women in the aquarobics group requested analgesia (a painkilling prescription medication), compared to 65% in the control group. This represents a 58% reduction in requests for the water aerobics group. Neonatal results from the study confirmed the well being of the newborn infants born to mothers who took part in the aquarobics.

Weight training, once heavily discouraged by doctors for pregnant women, is now recommended regularly under careful supervision. Don't push yourself too hard but focus instead on training with a low-moderate intensity program.

Q. Should I train my abdominal muscles every day to get them in shape?

A. Your abdominal muscles are similar to your other muscle groups and should be trained no more often than they are. While the goal of training most muscle groups is to tone, strengthen and add muscle size, the desired effect of ab training is to tone, strengthen and reduce the size of the area.

Many people mistakenly perform endless sets of high rep exercises in an effort to reduce the fat around their midsection. They believe that it is possible to burn fat by training the abs daily but that only leads to over training issues and, because the abdominals are a smaller muscle group, a lower amount of calories are burned compared to training larger muscle groups such as legs, back and chest.

The best method to train the abs is to do a reasonable amount of sets using moderate rep counts spread throughout 2-3 different exercises. Burn fat stores throughout the entire body by eating a healthy diet and doing a regular routine of cardio exercises such as swimming, biking and running/jogging. Try and do cardio on different training days than you do your strength training.

Q. Heavy or light weights-which is better for building muscle?

A. The traditional thought on building strength and muscle size is that it is necessary

for the trainee to use moderate to heavy weights to build strength and muscle size.
It was believed that weights that allowed 3-5 reps in an exercise generated primarily strength development without a lot of muscle increase. Repetitions in the range of 6-8 developed both strength and muscle size while repetitions of 10-12 contributed to muscle size without much strength.

Newer research seems to suggest that this may not be the case in all situations. McMaster University undertook a study that examined the relationship between light weights, heavy weights and intensity of effort as well as set count as it relates to muscle size gains.

They divided the test groups into three. One trained a muscle group using one set with 80% of their 1rm (one rep max). The second group did three sets of an exercise using a weight that was 80% of their 1rm. The third used a weight that was 30% of their 1rm, performed for three sets. After 10 weeks of training, three times a week, the heavy and light weight groups that trained with three sets gained significant amount of muscle while the group that trained with one set gained half the muscle that the others did. The group that used heavier weight for three sets gained a little more strength than the other two.

What does this show? This study demonstrated that lighter weights for higher reps tend to be just as effective as heavier weights for developing muscle size. Sarcoplasmic fluid in your muscles is largely responsible for muscle size gains and this fluid is expanded when you train using slightly higher reps that cause a deep burn.

If you are looking for strength gains, use a rep range of 3-5. If you are aiming to increase your muscle size primarily, do sets of 6-8 reps and 10-15 reps. The best method to incorporate these is to regularly alter your rep count to keep your muscles "off-balance" and end all of your sets at failure. This is the point where it is impossible to grind out even one more rep.

Q.I have been training with weights for a while now and haven't seen much results. What can I do to improve my results?

A. It's very hard to analyze what you may or may not be doing incorrectly from the little information you gave me but I will give you an outline of proper exercise performance and general diet guidelines to help you succeed. If you are attempting to gain muscle size you should increase your calories somewhat over what you need for maintenance. This differs substantially from person to person. If you have a skinny build and find it hard to gain weight then it will be necessary to increase your calories much more than a naturally larger individual.

Eat healthy calories such as fresh and cooked vegetables, lean protein and whole grains. With a proper diet you will gain mostly lean muscle with little or no fat but it is hard

to gain muscle and lose a lot of fat at the same time, so try to work on gaining
muscle and losing large amounts of fat at different times for best results.

As far as training goes, use both compound and isolation exercises but concentrate most of your program on compound movements such as squats, leg presses, bench presses, dead-lifts and such. These exercises use many different muscles at the same time as opposed to focusing efforts on one muscle group.

When you do your exercises make sure to use good form. If you swing or bounce the weight you will be risking severe injury and removing a good portion of the resistance from your muscles. Since proper weight resistance on your muscles is what stimulates growth, this defeats the purpose of exercising. Get adequate rest. While exercise stimulates growth, growth actually occurs while you are resting, as in deep sleep. Seven to eight hours per night is generally recommended.

Q. What are the elements of a well rounded exercise program?

A. The goal of every training program should be to develop great health, fitness, strength and muscle. This adds years to your life while making it easier to enjoy the activities of daily life. There are types of training that contribute to different areas of fitness more than others.

Aerobic training is the most popular type of training for getting in shape. Look at the high numbers of people jogging, running and swimming. This type of training aids greatly with fat loss and toning of your muscles. There are two major sub-types of aerobic training. Low intensity, which is best exemplified by jogging or brisk walking and HIIT, or high intensity, which follows an intense, 100% effort with either a complete rest or a low intensity "rest" period, where a slow paced aerobic exercise is performed for one minute before returning to the next all-out effort.

Strength training is an essential component of a successful training regimen. It helps by increasing lean muscle mass, strengthening tendons and connective tissue and thickens bones due to the weight-bearing effect. For the general public it is best to begin with a basic program to work all of the major muscle groups. Arm muscles usually get enough stimulation from chest and back training, so unless you're bodybuilding, direct arm training can be infrequent.

Weight training is great at counteracting muscle loss that naturally occurs as we age and staving off other serious health issues.

Stretching is important to help keep your muscles limber and injury-free. By keeping your body supple you avoid muscle pulls and sprains. It's important not to force your stretches or you will likely injure yourself, so be careful. Stretch your back and hamstrings by keeping your legs straight and bending forward and down as far as you can. Stretch your thighs by doing splits and your chest by holding onto a pole and leaning away in the opposite direction as far as you can.

Balance training is a great way to increase your stability, which helps prevent falls and other accidents and builds body awareness. To do this, stand on one leg while holding the other leg up. As you progress, begin extending the leg you're holding up out in front of you as high as you can. Next, hold it out to the side and finally out behind you.

To make this more challenging, hold your arms out to the side parallel to the floor as you do this exercise. Get creative and you will enjoy your exercise sessions more than ever, which can only benefit you.

Q. I don't have money for a gym membership? Can I still train effectively?

A. While gyms are an excellent place to train, many people want to get in shape but don't have the funds to pay for a gym membership. Is it possible to get in condition without going to a gym? Absolutely! There are many things you can do in your daily routine to help get yourself in shape.

Try and get in a brisk walk daily if the weather permits. Park farther away from the entrance at the mall and walk more. Take several laps around the mall, walking continuously without stopping at any stores. At work, take the stairs instead of the elevator. Mow the lawn with a push mower instead of a riding tractor, rake leaves, shovel dirt and stack firewood. Working in the house is great too, as long as you elevate your heart rate when you are doing the task.

Go to a fitness store near you and buy some inexpensive exercise tools such as dumbbells, kettlebells, a barbell and resistance tubes. These are versatile pieces of equipment that will allow you to train your entire body. Ask a trainer to help design a workout program for you using this equipment.

Kettlebells are old school weights that resemble a round ball with a handle attached. They were used many years ago by old-time strongmen and have made a comeback in popularity in recent years. There are many unique exercises that are available to train your entire body with a focus on functional strength development due to the entire body movements that are employed. Some examples are kettlebell swings, goblet squat and kettlebell clean and press.

Dumbbells are a close cousin to kettlebells and are just as versatile. They can be used to train the entire body with a wide variety of exercises including dumbbell rows, squats, bench presses, concentration curls, kickbacks and many more.

Barbells are a single bar version of dumbbells and can be used to train using both compound and isolation movements. While there are some drawbacks to using barbells for certain exercises, they are a very effective piece of equipment and are the most common training tool used today by fitness enthusiasts, bodybuilders, weightlifters and power-lifters Resistance tubes are very effective for isolating muscle groups and have

the advantage of increasing tension the further you stretch them. This maximizes   90
muscle fibers used during exercises, which increases the effectiveness of many of them.

Q. What is Phase Shift dieting?

A. While I recommend eating fairly clean all the time, I realize many of you will go on a "diet" at one time or another. What typically happens is you begin the diet by cutting bad carbs or calories and soon after the weight begins to drop off. This continues for a time and then suddenly- you hit a sticking point where no more fat is lost, often leading to frustration. What happens is your body has reacted to the reduced caloric consumption by slowing your metabolism down to preserve your fat stores in the event of starvation.

Is there a way to remedy this? Absolutely! We need to trick your body into believing that we are not going to starve it by altering our diet. To do this we are going to add phase-shift dieting. Once every 5 days increase your calories to nearly the point they were prior to your dieting for one day.

What this does is adjust your body to your old caloric level for the one day, which causes your body to increase your metabolism. The day after when you return to the reduced calories of your diet your metabolism will continue to burn calories at an elevated pace for several days. Repeat this sequence every 5 days during your diet to lose fat much faster than you would normally.

Proper Exercise, Diet and Good Sleep

We've all heard how important a good night's sleep is to our health and well-being. But what are some of the important benefits of getting a good night's sleep? Feeling refreshed the next day would have to be at the top of the list but having a good attitude and mood are a couple of additional benefits.

What constitutes a good night's sleep?

- Easy time falling asleep (you should be asleep within 20 minutes after going to bed)
- Uninterrupted sleep time of 6-7 hours
- Normal awakenings in between (normal is 1-2 awakenings in between to pee or re-hydrate)
- Fresh wake up next morning
- Energetic and positive attitude

One of the benefits of exercise is a better, sounder sleep. In a 16-week exercise study on people with chronic insomnia with a sedentary lifestyle, it was concluded that exercise has a positive effect on the quality and time of sleep. The participants followed a 30 minute exercise routine of light aerobics and running 3-4 times a week. The benefits weren't evident immediately but materialized over 16 weeks.

It wasn't necessary to follow a certain exercise program, aerobic and weight training had similar benefits. The important factor was the timing and intensity of the exercise. A suggestion was to avoid training before bedtime as the stimulation of the training could cause insomnia.

Exercise intelligence

An old saying states that jocks are dumb and nerds are out-of-shape geniuses. This may be inaccurate after all.

A new study shows that children who exercise more do better on mathematics and reading tests. "There is some truth that athletes may be the brightest," said Dr. Bob Rauner, author of the survey that compared standardized test scores of fourth- to eighth-grade children in public schools in Lincoln, Neb.

His study, published in the Journal of Pediatrics, showed that children who are more physically fit tended to do better in the math and reading tests than children who were less active and heavier. Rauner, a family physician for 15 years, who now runs Healthy Lincoln, a non-profit that advocates for childhood health, said his study was prompted by seeing a lot of obese kids. "We found that some of the most obese were in schools which did not even have recess."

He and colleagues from Lincoln Public Schools and Creighton University in Nebraska analyzed standardized tests for math and reading in 2010-2011, and compared them to students' aerobic fitness and body mass index (BMI).

The study found that physically fit children had a 2.4 times greater chance of passing math tests and a 2.2 times greater chance of passing reading tests compared with aerobically unfit children.

Training With Machines

While in the past most weight training enthusiasts used barbells and dumbbells exclusively, most make extensive use of machines in their training. Their use took off with the advent of Nautilus Machines, which were designed and produced by Arthur Jones. He worked with an associate, Ellington Darden, in developing exercise routines using the new machines.

He advocated three full-body workouts per week, with one rest day in-between. Each exercise was performed for one set only, two exercises per muscle group. They were done in a pre-exhaust fashion, that is an isolation exercise was done first followed by a compound one. An example of an isolation exercise for the chest is dumbbell flyes with the bench press an example of a compound one. Nautilus machines reached their peak in popularity during the early to mid eighties.

In more recent times, other manufacturers have also produced great pieces of equipment, many of them using cutting edge designs meant to train a muscle more closely along

its strength curve. Machines offer the fitness devotee a safe, effective tool
to train with. Many advanced training techniques including forced and negative reps, are much easier to do on machines.

The two types of machines are plate-loaded and selectorized. Plate-loaded machines' resistance levels are changed by adding or removing barbell plates while selectorized loads are changed by the insertion of a pin. I prefer, as do most people, the selectorized type because of the quick-change ability of the selector pin.

Power Rack Training for Legs

One of the great tools available at a complete gym is the power rack. Comprised of four upright posts with holes spaced one inch apart, a power rack enables the lifter to set safety pins eliminating the need for a spotter in the event of a missed lift.

Pin locations give the ability to train lifts at the weak link, or sticking point, to build strength and increase the maximum weight one is able to lift in an exercise.
A great muscle group to train with a power rack is the legs. An effective program to use is as follows:

- squats-5 sets of 15, 12,10,8,6 reps

Do the first three sets normally using full reps, lowering as far as you safely can. The fourth set should be done as a partial rep set. Set the pins so the lift begins at the mid point and do 8 reps from that point until the finish position of the squat. Change the pins so the lift begins at the bottom position and ends at the mid point and do 6 reps in that zone. The pin positions can be altered to train different points in the lift to work through sticking points.

Power racks have nearly limitless pin positions and are very helpful in loading up weight on big lifts and doing short rep partials.

Q. How much exercise should a woman do to see positive results?

A. It has been traditionally thought that the same amount and intensity of exercise is equally good for men and women but recent research indicates that may not be the case. This is especially true for people with type 2 diabetes.

Researchers took a look at the effects of walking exercise on both sexes and noticed that the men's heart rates recovered more quickly than did the women's after a steady state walking session. The people in the study all had type 2 diabetes and were grossly overweight.

While this study focused on walking, and not resistance training, it hi-lights
exercise's different effects on men and women. Women, it seems, need additional intensity and volume compared to a man's. More attention needs to be given to the time it takes to recover from an elevated heart rate. This gives a baseline for the measurement of an individual's condition.

Q.I play ice hockey. What tips can you offer me to help strengthen and condition myself for this sport?

A. Hockey is a vigorous sport with mostly non-stop action. This involves checking, skating very fast and taking quick shots at the net while attempting to score a goal. Hockey play is broken down into shifts, where each player goes onto the ice and plays hard then returns to the bench to take a break before returning to play.

The shift is usually 30-45 seconds in length, so the best way to train for this is to engage in high intensity training using a full intensity sprint or bicycle for two minutes then take a 90 second break before doing an additional two minute all-out effort. Initially, 2-3 cycles should be done and more should be added as conditioning improves. The best tools to use are a stationary bike and treadmill though sprinting on a padded track works well too.

To outline this program:
- warm-up with light cycling
- 100% effort cycling for two minutes
- light,low effort cycling for 90 seconds
- 100% effort cycling for two minutes
- light,low effort cycling for 90 seconds
- 100% effort cycling for two minutes
- light,low effort cycling for 90 seconds
- 100% effort cycling for two minutes
- light,low effort cycling for 90 seconds
- 100% effort cycling for two minutes
- light,low effort cycling for 90 seconds
- 100% effort cycling for two minutes
- cool down

This level is for the advanced hockey player. As mentioned, scale the number of HIIT cycles down to your present fitness level and work your way up. Don't do any additional cycles because that would diminish the advantage of this type of training. Focus instead on training harder not longer.

Q. Which grip is better to use while lifting weights, the neutral, pronated or supinated?

A. The grip used during training is an important factor as it can mean the
difference between success in using heavy weights in an exercise or failure to do so. One of the most important aspects in building more strength and muscle is to use heavier weights in an exercise or to complete a higher amount of reps. Both of these are crucial to overloading the muscle. In upper body exercises grip variation changes the angle of the elbows offering a different stimulation to the muscles.

Using the dumbbell curl as an example, if you use the normal palms-up grip, the weight supinates as the little finger goes toward your shoulder. This makes the curl use both actions of the biceps. One is to bring the forearm to the shoulder and the other is to turn the wrist outward to the shoulder. If you use a neutral grip, there is no supination but the grip makes the curl feel more natural and is easier on the joints. As a result more weight is able to be used in the exercise.

Chin-ups are usually done with an overhand, palms-outward wide grip on the chin-up bar. If the grip is changed to a medium width, palms-facing grip more reps can be completed. This is because the angle of the elbows was changed.

The next time you're in the gym, try varying your grip to get the most out of your training.

Power Factor Training

There is a system of weight training that gauges the intensity by the total amount of weight lifted in a given amount of time. If you are training for 45 minutes and have lifted a total of 1200 pounds cumulatively in all exercises and the next workout lift a total of 1500 pounds, the analysis would be that the second session was more intense than the first.

But is this the correct method to judge the intensity of a workout?

Many times you will read that to increase the intensity of a workout you need to add weight. This is only partially true as the intensity of an exercise is increased by training harder not necessarily heavier. In fact, many times training can be made more intense by training with lighter weight!

The way to do this is to use a HIT technique called drop sets. With drop sets an initial set is done to failure. Enough weight is stripped off the barbell or reduced on a selectorized machine to allow an additional set to be done to failure. These are called mini-sets.

This is continued until a total of 6-8 mini-sets are completed. This constitutes one total set. Because all mini-sets are done to failure the intensity is high. To increase it further, add forced reps at the end of some mini-sets.

A sample workout for biceps is:

- cable curls-1 total set of 1 mini-set of 8 reps,2nd mini-set of 6 reps, 3rd mini-set of 6 reps, 4th mini-set of 5 reps, 5th mini-set of 4 reps, 6th mini-set of 4 reps
- concentration curls-1 total set of 1 mini-set of 8 reps,2nd mini-set of 6 reps, 3rd mini-set of 6 reps, 4th mini-set of 5 reps, 5th mini-set of 4 reps, 6th mini-set of 4 reps

As mentioned, reduce the weight quickly between mini-sets to allow completion of the desired reps. Don't rest at all between mini-sets, pausing long enough to change the weight only. So you see, intensity can be increased by decreasing the weight used during an exercise.

Q. What is the best way or ways to avoid injury when restarting a sport in the spring? I play a lot of golf once the weather gets nice.

A. This is a common issue for sports enthusiasts who don't properly maintain fitness levels in the off-season and certainly includes weekend warriors such as yourself. This reinforces the importance of maintaining an adequate level of conditioning to both live a healthy life and enjoy partaking in sports such as tennis and golf.

A fitness program designed to both prevent injuries and help provide sports enjoyment should include stretching, aerobic and strength training. Some of the common areas for injuries are the shoulders, elbows and hips, therefore some of the training focus should be on strengthening these areas. There are exercises that will build up these areas involving the use of dumbbells and bands.

For the shoulders hold a light dumbbell in each hand and rotate it in a clockwise motion while holding it at shoulder height to train the rotator cuff area. Reverse direction and do a series of rotations in that direction. For the hips attach a cable from a cable machine to your ankle and do a series of side, rear and frontal extensions to develop strength and flexibility. To strengthen the elbow region use dumbbell curls, strength band triceps extensions and wrist rotations using an iron grip twisting tool ,available at sporting goods stores.

Regaining Conditioning

After an injury or illness it often becomes difficult to bounce back to your former self, especially if it is after a prolonged recuperative period. After assessing present conditioning, begin training again slowly with an abbreviated program.

Use low intensity aerobic training including walking, bicycling or treadmill exercise, working up gradually to a more intense program. A short weight training routine including basic exercises is great. Movements like leg extensions, leg presses, bench presses, dips, presses, curls, triceps presses, sit-ups or crunches and dumbbell rows are ideal. Avoid any of these exercises if there is an injury present in the particular muscle involved in the performance of the exercise.

Dumbbells are great tools to use as they are safer than barbells because of spotter issues for certain barbell exercises and the reduced stress on the joints from dumbbell use. Exercise machines are an even better bet because they eliminate the need to balance the weight and are easiest on joints and allow better weight control.

A good, simple program to begin with is:

- leg presses-1 set of 15 reps
- bench presses-1 set of 10 reps
- rows-1 set of 10 reps
- presses-1 set of 10 reps
- curls-1 set of 12 reps
- triceps extensions-1 set of 12 reps
- ab crunches-1 set of 20 reps

This basic program trains every major muscle group using a reduced program for overall conditioning and strength gain.

Elderly Muscle

New UCLA research suggests that the more muscle mass older Americans have, the less likely they are to die prematurely. This is part of growing evidence that overall body composition -- and not the widely used body mass index, or BMI -- is a better predictor of mortality.

The study is the culmination of previous UCLA research led by Dr. Preethi Srikanthan, an assistant clinical professor in the endocrinology division at the David Geffen School of Medicine at UCLA, that found that building muscle mass is important in decreasing metabolic risk.

The degree of muscle mass one has in his/her body depends on many factors, including eating habits, genetics, protein intake and training to name a few. The metabolism tends to increase as muscle tissue is added to the body because muscle mass burns more calories than any other tissue.

Muscle, while requiring a lot of energy and resources to maintain, provides the body 97
with additional protection for the internal organs in the event of impact resulting from an
accident. People with the most muscle mass tend to be more energetic and often lead
very active lifestyles, all of which tend to lengthen lifespan.

HIIT Cycle Training

When you typically think of aerobic training you naturally think of jogging, swimming
and other similar exercises. But recently a newer form of aerobic training has been
gaining in popularity.

HIIT, or high intensity interval training, differs from low-moderate intensity aerobic
training such as jogging in that it condenses all of the effort into short bursts of
maximum effort with brief rest periods in between.

Typically people who jog do so for 5 miles or more 3-5 times per week using a low to
moderate pace. This is considered low intensity aerobic training. If enough effort is put
forth, this training can result in substantial fat loss if an appropriate diet is undertaken.
But research has shown that the same amount or more calories are burned during a HIIT,
High Intensity Interval Training session even though a session lasts, in many cases, only
15-20 minutes, two-three times per week.

To try a HIIT version of aerobic training perform the following routine using running
(sprinting) as an example:

- Warm up with brisk walking for 2 minutes followed by a moderate jog for one
  minute.
- Sprint with as near 100% effort as you can for 20 seconds
- Walk briskly for 1 ½ minutes
- Sprint for 20 seconds
- Walk briskly for 1 ½ minutes

Repeat this for one more cycle. After the last cycle do a cool down period of moderate
walking for two minutes. Do this training twice per week during the initial month. It's a
good idea to have three rest days between workouts to allow your muscles and central
nervous system time to fully recuperate. If you find that you are dragging when you
attempt to repeat the training, add a rest day before resuming. This will allow you to
build up your tolerance for this type of training over a safe time-frame. During the
second month increase your sessions by doing a total of 5 cycles per session. Repeat this
routine three times per week.

A very effective method for increasing the effectiveness of this type of training is to vary

both the rest periods and the short bursts of effort. For instance, try doing a
15-second sprint with a one-minute rest period in between or a 10 second sprint with a 45-second rest period. This is a great way to keep your exercise interesting and avoid boredom. Set goals for yourself and remember you get results based on the effort put forth!

Building Muscle Over 40

When young bodybuilders train with weights they are able to push harder, increasing the weights nearly every workout. As the years go by, they soon realize their body has changed- they may slow down a bit as the aches and pains creep in. The bodybuilder over 40 typically has been training for decades and more than likely has amassed a few injuries along the way.

The question is-are older bodybuilders still able to make gains in strength and size safely? The answer is Yes! Training routines will need to be altered a bit-using moderate poundages instead of bar-bending loads. Of utmost importance is proper form in all exercises to place the resistance on the muscle while avoiding tearing ligaments and tendons. This advice is best heeded by bodybuilders of all ages to develop muscles to the fullest while avoiding injuries.

Train your entire body regularly to maintain strength and conditioning throughout, using weight levels that continue to tax your muscles and strive to add weight to the bar or machine at every workout. Use a varied workout routine-changing it often to keep it fresh and stimulating your muscles.

HIIT, High Intensity Interval Training should be used to maximize your cardiovascular conditioning. After a thorough warm-up, do a 20-second burst of all-out peddling on a stationary or traditional bike followed by a one minute low intensity peddling period. Do four of these when beginning, increasing to 7-8 later on.

The following HIT routine will prove to be effective for the over 40 bodybuilder:

Chest
- Pek dek machine flyes-1x15
- Incline dumbbell bench press-1x10
- Machine dips-1x6

Back
- Stiff-arm pull-downs-1x12
- One-arm dumbbell rows-1x8
- Medium-grip lat pull-downs-1x10

Legs
- Leg lunges with dumbbell-1x15 each leg
- Leg press-1x12
- Barbell squat-1x10

Shoulders
- Seated machine or dumbbell side delt raise-1x12
- Dumbbell press-1x8

Biceps
- Concentration curl-1x12
- Palms-facing lat pull-downs-1x8

Triceps
- Standing cable push-downs-1x12
- Standing bar dips-1x10

Abs
- Machine ab crunches-1x25
- Leg raises on flat bench-1x20

Forearms
- Barbell wrist curls-1x25
- Reverse wrist curls-1x25

Give this basic HIT training routine a try in your next workout cycle. End most sets at the point of muscular failure using moderate level weights.

Does The Way A Muscle Feel After a Workout Determine If Your Workout Was A Success?

Does the way your muscle feel after a workout dictate how successful you were in developing sufficient stimulus to cause your muscles to grow? Not necessarily. While delayed soreness is an indication of micro tears in muscle, which are necessary to cause the body to overcompensate and build more muscle tissue after a workout, it doesn't indicate if proper training protocols were followed during the workout.

For instance, one could get on a stationary cycle and peddle at a moderate pace for an extended period of time and get sore in the leg muscles a day or two later. But that training does little to build muscle. It will build endurance but offers insufficient resistance to stimulate muscle growth.

The trick is to find the proper intensity level,number of reps or time under tension and resistance level to use in your training to get optimum results. One of the ways to do this

is to do an analysis of muscle fiber content in each muscle group. That way 100
you will be able to use the proper tut for each muscle group. A muscle fiber analysis is
done in the following way:

Select an isolation exercise and strictly perform an arbitrary number of repetitions at a
moderate to slow speed, e.g., 6-12 repetitions, at about a 5/5 cadence (make certain the
TUT is at least 60 seconds; rest approximately three minutes then complete a second set
of that exercise with the same weight. In both sets train to muscular failure and record
your TUT. If the TUT in the second set is 50% or less than the first set, that muscle
group is predominantly fast twitch (since the muscle lost so much strength). If you lose
less than 15% TUT, maintained or even increased your TUT in the second set (which is
possible), that muscle group is predominantly slow twitch. Anything between these two
figures represent a mixed fiber type, whose ratios reflect the degree of TUT reduction.

Now that you have determined muscle fiber type and ideal tut, or number of
reps,whichever method you use, it is time to develop an ideal training regimen to
maximize muscular development. If your muscle is mostly fast twitch, use a tut of 45-60
seconds per set. If it is slow twitch, use a tut of 90-120 seconds. If it falls in-between use
a tut of 65-90 seconds.

Some important points to take away from this is to use:

- Ideal tut or reps for each muscle fiber type/group
- proper amount of resistance to cause muscular failure or exhaustion with this
  rep count
- constantly attempt to use more weight every workout
- get the proper amount of rest
- train the right amount and none extra to avoid over training

The Hack Squat

The Forgotten Exercise That Packs Muscle On Your Legs Fast!

One of the most overlooked muscle groups in a beginning bodybuilder's training
program is legs. They don't impress like the chest and arms so beginners make a
common mistake and avoid training them, not realizing the overall high growth effect
the leg muscles exert over the entire body. It has been demonstrated in recent research
that if intense leg training is done prior to arm training in a workout session, the overall
growth effect on the arms is magnified. This is a result of human growth hormone
being released because of the size of the leg muscles.

The best way to capitalize on this benefit is to construct your training sessions so your 'difficult' body parts are trained immediately after training legs. There are quite a few good exercises to develop the legs including squats,front squats, leg extensions, leg curls and stiff-legged dead-lifts Hack squats are not nearly as popular as these other exercises but are an effective muscle builder.

This lift was named after George Hackenschmidt, an early 20th-century strongman, wrestler and writer. He advocated this exercise because of its ability to develop leg strength quickly while avoiding excessive hip development common with barbell squats. In his book , The Way To Live, he mentions that the exercise was named after him. In North America the name Hack Squat is the term most often used when describing this exercise.

Steve Reeves, of Hercules and Mr. America fame, began using the hack squat to develop a sweep in his thigh muscles while avoiding hip enlargement and even developed a piece of equipment to allow him to perform the movement more effectively. Several photos I've seen show him training in Vic Tanny's gym in California, near the famed Muscle Beach.

But what is the best training program to use with hack squats? First, let's look at proper exercise technique. There are some really great hack squat machines on the market which remove the balance problem encountered when using a barbell. But let's assume you don't have access to those and train with barbells and dumbbells. After electing to use either a barbell or dumbbell, place your heels on a block, keeping your legs close together. Hold the weight behind you and lower yourself until your buttocks comes close to touching your heels. Press yourself up with your legs as you exhale. Avoid locking out at the top of the movement. Repeat until hitting muscular failure.

As mentioned previously, there are numerous hack squat machines on the market. Most have bars for loading barbell plates but a couple have selectorized weight stacks for ease of changing the weight.

The reasons I like hack squats are the absence of heavy resistance on your back and shoulders compared to regular squats, ability to train thigh muscles while limiting excessive hip development and the lack of weight balancing when using a hack squat machine. Another great feature of this exercise is the stimulation it gives your hamstring muscles, which is a result of the deep descent I recommend. Give this exercise a try and you will be adding a new tool for quick leg muscle development.

A standard training routine for legs using hack squats is listed below. The routine is based on the HIT,high intensity training protocol so be sure and put 100% effort into each set by taking them to complete muscular failure and resting minimally between

sets:
warm-up
hack squats-1x12
leg extensions-1x15 (3 forced reps at the end of the set to be performed every other workout session)
leg curls-1x15
standing calf raises-1x20

Building Your Shoulders With Different Variations Of The Press

The press was one of three lifts in Olympic lifting until 1972 when it was deleted due to hardship in judging. I feel it's easier to judge than the other two lifts, the snatch and clean and jerk. But enough of that-let's get down to ways to use the press to build muscle! There are many different tools which can be used to perform this popular exercise- dumbbells,barbells, bands and machines. Each one of these offers it's distinct advantages, which will be briefly outlined here.

Strict Military Barbell Press
This is the most popular press and is a very effective exercise to pack muscle on the delts. Load a barbell up with the desired weight and stand or sit and press the bar overhead. The downside is you're locked into a straight groove.

Dumbbell Press
The use of dumbbells allows for much greater variety. Instead of being locked into a set pattern, the dumbbells can be rotated to activate surrounding muscles,which are often referred to as the 'stabilizer' muscles.

Selectorized Press Machine
These allow quick and easy weight selection because they have a stack of weight plates with a quick-change selector pin. A well-designed machine will force you to use the appropriate range of motion for the exercise based on scientific studies. These are great for safe control of movement while doing forced reps and negatives.

Smith Press
The Smith machine adds a measure of safety to the barbell press but has a trade-off. A barbell slides in a fixed plane along a pair of guide rods. There are pairs of pins which allow the bodybuilder to place the bar at many different locations. There is a safety catch which brakes the descent of the bar if dropped. Many different exercises can be done with the Smith machine including the barbell squat,press and triceps press. Exercises must follow a very limited plane due to the bar guides. This is a disadvantage as it often places the bar in an unnatural position during a given movement.

Band Presses

One of the newer training tools available,and one I really find useful, is bands. Developed for use in power-lifting training, these have proven to be great for building tension as the range of motion increases during an exercise. I find them very effective for static holds and partial reps. They are available in many different resistant levels.

Behind-The-Neck Press

This exercise stresses the shoulders in a way different than the front press does. This can be a great way to provide a new stimulus but bodybuilders must be conscious of shoulder impingement and the increase of injury incidence. To do this exercise, load a bar with the desired weight. After placing the hands at a slightly wider than shoulder width and the bar behind the neck, press it straight overhead.

Ways To Increase The Results From Your Training

There are many different methods to magnify the results obtained from training. As a HIT practitioner, I have used many of these and have devised several of my own.

Forced reps-These are done at the end of a set after hitting muscular failure. Have a friend provide enough assistance to allow the completion of 1-3 additional reps. This is great for really upping the intensity of a workout.

Negative reps-Load a bar with 140% of the weight you normally use in a set of presses. After your partner lifts the weights to the top, you lower the bar to an eight count. These are great strength and muscle builders.

Burn reps-After completing a set to failure, do a series of short,pulse reps until you feel a deep burn. The range of motion should not exceed six inches.
These will allow us to maximize delt and trap muscle growth with the proper application.

The following routines are great for adding muscle and power using the HIT protocol:

Burn Reps/Forced Reps

- Seated side dumbbell lateral raises-1x12+burn reps to failure

no rest

- Incline dumbbell presses-1x8+3 forced reps

Forced Reps

- Bent-over cable lateral raises-1x12+2 forced reps

no rest

- Standing dumbbell press-1x6+4 forced reps

Pure Negative Reps

- Machine press-1x8(partner lifts machine arm to top)

10-second rest

- Front dumbbell raise-1x8(partner lifts dumbbells to top)

These three routines should be used consistently with a constant attempt to add weight in small increments. Weekly increases of 1-2 pounds really add up over a year's time, while avoiding the Golgi tendon reflex,which is the body's way to avoiding severe injuries to muscles and tendons during heavy lifting.

Do the first routine for one month and evaluate your progress. You should train your delts once every 7-10 days to allow them to receive the necessary rest. If you repeat training too soon, your muscles won't be fully recuperated and your growth will have been impeded. The gym is where growth is stimulated but muscles grow when at rest. The forced rep routine should be used during month two, with the pure negative used during month three.

The 10-Minute Grip-Strengthening Workout To Build Crushing Strength!

With all the various wrist straps being used by power-lifters,bodybuilders and weightlifters today, you might think a powerful grip is unnecessary. But athletes in many different sports, including weightlifters and power-lifters, need a powerful grip to succeed in their chosen sport.

Many articles are written about developing a powerful, well-developed pair of upper arms, but not much is written about building serious power and strength in the lower arms. For now, we are going to be focusing on the different components of a strong grip and ways to strengthen them. This is especially important to the aspiring athlete, who may not be interested in competing in the local bodybuilding contest but desires to ratchet up to the next level in his/her chosen sport.

The forearm muscle group is the one responsible for grip strength. There are several functions of the forearm muscles including gripping objects, curling the fist upward and lifting the hand backward in a reverse motion. Therefore, we have to train each of these areas for complete forearm development.

Pinch gripping a barbell plate is a great exercise to build overall grip strength. Begin by pinching the edge of a barbell plate using the thumb and all fingers and lifting it up to thigh height. Hold the plate as long as possible. Gradually increase the weight of the plate lifted.

One of my favorite tools to build a powerful grip is an iron gripper. Avoid the ones in sporting goods stores as they are weak and don't provide enough resistance for a good

workout. A complete line of pro grippers includes units with resistance levels
from 50 lbs all the way up to 500 lbs.! An alternative to the gripper is the common tennis ball. Use an old ball and squeeze it as hard as you can for a count of 15 seconds before resting. Repeat.

A series of cable wind-ups builds the overall strength needed in the forearm for a strong grip. Use one from a sporting goods store or make your own from a wooden handle. Drill a hole in the middle and insert a six foot rope through it and tie the end. Attach a quick coupler on the other end. After clipping on a barbell plate, wind it up until it touches the handle. Unwind and repeat.

No forearm/grip development training program would be complete without reverse barbell curls. Keep your elbows firmly against your sides throughout the exercise. Using smooth movement and a palms-down grip, lift the weight up in a circular motion until it is at shoulder height.

Now that I've explained the different functions of the forearm muscles with relation to grip strength, and the different exercises to develop them, I will outline an effective program for the athlete to follow to maximize the development of a strong grip.

Session 1
- Reverse Barbell Curls- 1x 15 reps
- Gripper squeezes-1x 25 overhand, straight grip

Session 2
- Barbell Wrist Curls-1x15(palms-facing up)
- Tennis Ball Squeezes-1x25 each hand

During the initial two workouts use weights that are not too taxing for the muscles. After that increase the weights used every session until maximal effort is needed to complete the required rep counts. Continue adding weight to each exercise every session.

Strengthening The Lower Back

An often overlooked part of the physique is the lower back, or lumbar. Much attention is given to the more visible upper back at the expense of its bottom portion. Many bodybuilders focus their training on the abs and build up strength and conditioning in this area. This also causes an imbalance if the lower back isn't trained as well.

If this continues, it can cause lower-back injuries severe enough to end bodybuilding careers. So bodybuilders need to take some advice from their power-lifting counterparts and focus training efforts on building size and strength in this important muscle group.

That leads us to the question-how best to train the lower back? Should I 106
do mostly medium-weight isolation moves or power-building compound exercises like dead-lifts?

The answer is to do both. It's important to build up the muscles with isolation exercises but you need to "tie-in" these muscles with surrounding ones and build functional strength. We will be using routines with both types of exercises and some with one or the other.

List of exercises:

Good Mornings-This isolation movement is a great one for focusing exclusively on the lower back muscles. Place a barbell with a moderate weight behind your neck. Bend forward at the waist while keeping your knees locked. Continue until horizontal with the floor. Return to the upright position before repeating.

Roman Chair Hyper-extensions-Another great way to isolate your lower back and build up strength. Lie face down on a roman chair, placing your feet under the legs to hold yourself in place. With your hands locked behind your head, lift your upper body up as far as you can go and pause for a second before lowering.

Seated Machine Lower Back Extensions-Sit in an extension machine after selecting a moderate weight. Slowly extend back until perpendicular with the floor. Pause for one second and return.

Barbell Dead-lift- Load a barbell with the desired weight. Use either a standard grip or an over-under one. Bend your knees while crouching down. Your feet should be wider than shoulder-width. Using your back and leg muscles, lift the bar up and backward until your knees are locked and you're bent slightly backward. A pair of dumbbells can be used as an alternative.

Deficit Dead-lift- Begin by standing on a large block that's approx. 3 inches in height. Bend down and grip the bar with an over-under grip. Do a dead-lift using proper form. This form gives some extra range-of-motion to the lift.

Seated Cable Back Extensions- Sit in front of a cable machine while grasping a double rope handle in front of your forehead. Lean back against the resistance until fully-extended. Pause for one second, return.

HIT Routine

Dead-lift-1x8
rest 10 seconds

Roman chair hyper-extensions-1x15+4, 10-second holds at end of set. 107
    (To do the holds,
extend to the top and hold for 10 seconds,rest 10 seconds, repeat. Continue until four
holds have been completed.)

Power-lifting Dead-lift Routine
Dead-lift-6x8,6,4,3,2,2 (Rest three minutes between sets. Add weight as you reduce the
reps on each set. Use at or near max weight on each set.)
Roman Chair Hyper-extensions-4x12,10,8,3 (Rest three minutes between sets. Hold a
weight plate behind your head to add weight.)
Good Mornings-2x10,6 (Rest one minute between sets.)

Things to concentrate on:

Use relatively slow, deliberate movements with strict form. While dead-lifts require
faster movement than machine extensions do, avoid fast,jerky movement to prevent
injuries. Add weight to the bar or machine in small increments to avoid activating the
Golgi Tendon, which limits the muscle's ability to contract against resistance by nerve
deactivation. This is the body's way of avoiding damaging injuries to tendon,ligaments
and muscles during strenuous activities. Record weights used and repetitions during
each exercise. This is the only way to set goals and achieve them.

Focus on the muscle to increase the mind-muscle connection. After you have been training for awhile, you will be able to make the weight feel heavier on the muscle being
trained by increasing the efficiency of the neuromuscular system.

Why Bodybuilders Are More Muscular Than Power-lifters

There are a number of reasons for this. First off, the training styles of bodybuilders and
power-lifters differ greatly. Bodybuilders perform exercises with a rep range of 6-12 for
most sets, while power-lifters use 1-5. The goal of power-lifters is the development of
explosive power and strength with a lesser concern over the addition of muscle mass.
Bodybuilders, on the other hand, are principally concerned with the addition of muscle
mass and less with the development of strength.

Training protocols are practiced by each to reach their respective goals. For power-
lifters, this means using low rep ranges, which have been shown to develop maximum
strength with less muscle mass. Bodybuilders use moderate rep counts , which have
been shown to develop strength but yield more muscle mass. There are several
reasons for this. A muscle grows by muscle cell damage being repaired with the use of
raw materials, i.e. nutrients such as protein,vitamins,etc. The blood pump that results
from higher rep training is great for bringing blood into the muscle due to occlusion that

occurs with each rep. This blood is full of the nutrients needed for growth 108
and repair. Some studies show that the added blood volume exerts a hydraulic pressure on the muscle, stimulating it to grow larger and increases protein synthesis.

Higher reps stimulate growth of tendons and other tissue surrounding muscles, adding a little size. Slow-twitch fibers in the muscle, while responsible for less than half of a muscle's size, are stimulated to grow by higher reps. These fibers use oxygen as fuel and are geared for endurance so the longer time under tension of bodybuilding training is ideal for them. Low rep sets offer no stimulation for these fibers to grow because of short set duration.

Getting back to a previous point, when a routine is done where the muscles burn and are fatigued, there is a condition called muscle swelling. The fibers in the muscle being trained are exposed to sufficient stress to cause them to become inflamed due to small micro tears in the muscle. This stress causes the body to call for new muscle growth to combat the onslaught. Routines with minimal rest, common among bodybuilders, cause this. Longer rest periods between sets, such as done by power-lifters, doesn't exert enough trauma to elicit this reaction.

So, if you are looking to increase your strength with less of a focus on hypertrophy, train like a power-lifter, using sets of 1-5 reps with maximum weights. If you are aiming for larger muscles and a bodybuilders physique, train like a bodybuilder, using higher rep counts and more varied exercises with a shorter rest period between sets.

Training For Bodybuilding, Figure And Power-lifting Competitions

Have you ever wondered what it would be like to train for a power-lifting, bodybuilding or fitness competition? As you can image it takes strict discipline, devotion and determination to be successful at the regional level let alone at the national level, as the caliber of competitors has really increased in recent years. There are strict training and dieting regimens for bodybuilding and fitness competitions and specialized equipment needed for modern-day power-lifting meets.

There are many new nutritional supplements available to help make your training more successful by feeding nutrients to your muscles and many new training methods and techniques to make an athlete more competitive.

Bodybuilding

The first sport we will take a look at is the sport of bodybuilding. Some say that it isn't really a sport at all because the competitors aren't shooting a puck, dunking a basketball or hitting a home run. Not so says local pro bodybuilder, Kurt Giles. Kurt has been training for more than 20 years in an effort to build his physique by adding muscle, 109 shaping it and purging it of excess fat. His efforts have won him several regional bodybuilding titles and a pro card most of them with the NABBA, an international bodybuilding federation, known for producing tough competition.

I recently asked Kurt to outline his contest preparations with me in an effort to see just what it takes to become a bodybuilding champion. When preparing for a particular contest, Kurt establishes an outline consisting of diet, training and posing routine practice. He uses this to time his preparation, which is based on the number of weeks before the upcoming contest.

For instance, 12-16 weeks before the contest, he puts himself on a strict diet consisting of chicken, tuna and vegetables. He only eats carbs right after he finishes training to replenish his energy which was used up during training. Six weeks before the contest he begins cutting all sodium from his diet. Two weeks before the contest he adds sodium back to his diet and is now eating only a small amount of carbs.

He spaces out his meals so he is eating 5-6 meals a day, something that many health experts recommend for weight (fat) loss. For the final 11/2 weeks he increases his sodium and water intake, drinking three gallons of water daily. His schedule looks like this: Week prior-Wednesday through Saturday he drinks three gallons, Sunday two gallons, Monday and Tuesday 1/2 gallon, Wednesday 1/4 gallon and Thursday and Friday he only sips water. This is in an effort to "trick" his body into thinking that he is still drinking large amounts of water.

The morning of the show he will eat a fair amount of a simple carb such as pizza. This pulls water into his muscles making them appear larger while leaving little water under his skin. "This really shows the cuts and striations of my muscles." Says Kurt. "Many guys misjudge the timing of this carb loading prep and end up looking puffy and fat even though they may have a low fat percentage."

He takes several supplements though all of them are in powder form instead of pills. He takes L-Glutamine, fish oil, L-Arginine and BCAA's but stays away from Creatine as he says that causes too much water retention right before a contest. L-Glutamine is great for muscle recuperation, L-Arginine helps the pump and BCCA's or branched chain amino acids are the building blocks of muscle fibers.

His training* consists of 12-16 total sets using 4-5 different exercises for larger muscle groups such as legs, chest and back while he uses 6-12 sets divided into 2-4 exercises for arms, shoulders, abdominals and calves. All of this keeps him in the gym for 1-2 hours per training day. Most sets are taken until he hits muscular failure, when he is unable to complete any more full reps in the set. The week of the show he trains his legs on

Wednesday for the last time and ends all training on Thursday so that he has time to fully recuperate for the show.

Kurt stressed to me the importance of proper posing practice to harden the muscles and make his posing during the show seem effortless and natural. To do this he practices posing for 30 minutes twice per week.

Bodybuilding shows are divided into two parts: prejudging and the evening show. During the prejudging the competitors are evaluated by the judges for size, vascularity, symmetry and conditioning, or low fat levels. This is done by using a round of mandatory poses using side-by-side comparisons of the athletes. Kurt stressed the importance of finding which poses make your physique look the best and making sure to angle those poses toward the judges to allow them to see your muscles to your best advantage.

Two days prior to the show he begins to apply spray tan to darken his skin, which would look pale under the bright stage lights otherwise. Right before hitting the stage he sprays Pam on his skin and spreads it out to give his body the shiny appearance one needs to effectively showcase your muscles. All of the scoring is done during the prejudging and the winner chosen. The evening show is where the competitors get a chance to show off for the crowd using their own custom posing routine, which lasts for 90 seconds and is set to the music of their choice.

Figure

Brenda Brysons is a former female bodybuilding and fitness champion and has even been a promoter of local bodybuilding contests. She now trains other women to prepare them for figure and bikini competitions.

Her program begins twenty weeks prior to her client's show. She has her client eat very clean, in other words, a diet consisting of six meals per day of whole foods and a couple of protein shakes. She feels that it is very important to eat healthy fats because of their ability to help rid the body of excess fat. At this point she has her client begin 40 minutes of cardio per day in addition to weight training.

Training takes place in the gym using six training days in a row followed by one rest day. Each muscle group is trained using five exercises with four sets of 8-12 rep each. At 12 weeks before the show, diet consists of four ounces of lean meat, ¼ cup of carbs and one teaspoon of healthy fat such as fish oil or olive oil.

Cardio takes place for 45 minutes in the morning and 45 minutes after the last meal of the day. The step mill is the tool of choice for this as it effectively works the buttocks and legs, two difficult areas for women.

Posing practice is important in her program as well and takes place for twenty minutes each day to make sure each pose is hit correctly and becomes natural. Two days before the show Brenda applies Protan, which is a type of dye designed to build a dark, full tan so the competitor isn't washed out under the stage lights, to her client.

The night before the show the diet consists of a 12 oz. NY Strip steak with one white potato and the morning of the show two pancakes and a 4 oz. Steak are eaten while avoiding the intake of any water.

She stresses the need to make a strong impression for the judges because each competitor only gets 60 seconds to pose during the prejudging. All of the judging takes place during the prejudging while the evening show is there for the fitness competitor to show off her figure to the crowd using a 90 second routine.

Power-lifting

Mike Spellman was always a naturally gifted power-lifter, having bench pressed 405 lbs. while in 10th grade. After he got bitten by the "iron bug" he enthusiastically began training and shifted his attention toward power-lifting and worked hard at improving his bench press, dead-lift and squat lifts.

The world of power-lifting has changed dramatically in the years since Mike began training with the addition of "shirted" competitions which use single, double or three ply bench shirts that fit really tight on the lifter's chest and compress while the bar is lowered in the bench press causing a spring effect which helps the lifter lift more weight. Though this is a very popular piece of equipment there has been a strong resurgence of non-equipped lifting called Raw Power-lifting. While Mike does use a bench shirt to remain competitive during a meet he prefers to lift raw in the bench press but regularly uses a squat suit and a full body suit, which helps him lift more weight in the squat and dead-lift

While getting ready for a meet Mike does the following training* routine:

Bench press
Several warm-up sets in the bench pres
Bench press- 1 set of 10-14 reps, 1 set of 6-8 reps, 1 set of 4 reps
Decline bench press- 1 set 12-15 reps, 1 set 6-8 reps, 1 set 4-6 reps
Cable crossovers- 1 set 8-12 reps
Squats
- Several warm-up sets using leg extensions

- Leg extensions- 1 set 8-12 reps, 1 set 4-6 reps
- Squats- 2 sets of 50 reps, 1 set 20-25 reps, 1 set 4 reps

All squats are full range of motion with the descent portion going down until his buttocks are almost touching the floor.

- Leg presses- 1 set 8-12 reps

Super-setted with

- Leg extensions- 1 set 8-12 reps and stiff-legged dead-lifts- 1 set 8-12 reps
- Calf raises- 1 set 12-15 reps

Dead-lifts

- Several warm-up sets
- Dead-lifts- 1 set 10-14 reps, 1 set 6-8 reps, 1 set 4 reps
- Mid-height pulls in power rack- 1 set 10-14 reps, 1 set 6-8 reps, 1 set 4 reps
- Barbell rows- 1 set 10-14 reps, 1 set 6-8 reps, 1 set 4 reps

There are strict rules for lifts during competition such as no bouncing of the bar during a bench press, going below knee level during the squat and no reversal of movement during the dead-lift For more information on the technical requirements and more visit http://www.usapowerlifting.com/aboutus/USAPL%20Rulebook-2013_1.pdf.
*Not HIT Routines

The information regarding contest preparation for these competitions isn't a reflection on high intensity training as they are using traditional medium-high volume training. They do outline the contest preparations that most competitors use.

Thank you for purchasing this book. If the suggestions contained within are followed carefully your results will definitely increase. Remember, the more effort you put into your training the more you will receive from it.

For more detailed information my complete 9-book collection is available for purchase at: https://drhitscomplete9bookseries.blogspot.com/

My books are available for purchase individually at: https://drhitshighintensitybody-building.blogspot.com/